The Entrepreneurial Mind and Spirit

Jonathan Jay Belding

The Entrepreneurial Mind and Spirit

An A to Z Guide to the Practice of Success

The Entrepreneurial Mind and Spirit
An A to Z Guide to the Practice of Success

© 2023 Jonathan Jay Belding

Prepared for publication by www.greatwriting.org

ISBN: 979-8-9864349-3-3

Cover design: www.greatwriting.org
Book layout and design: www.greatwriting.org

The purpose of this book is:

To inform of and suggest emulating the common traits, characteristics, and work habits entrepreneurs practice and employ which can be of benefit to all;

To encourage adopting leadership roles as they emerge, and to suggest integrating a servanthood-based model or style;

To infuse, and energize readers to couraeously ventuer forth in life as they seek their passion and purpose.

This work is dedicated to all the entrepreneurially minded and spirited people who have informed and inspired me, especially my wife and partner, Barbara.

From the Author's Pen

The author notes that over his decades of experience in business, he has read widely and appreciated the wisdom of many others in business, often writing down their key ideas. In the event that there are quotations or allustions that are not fully attributed in footnotes, the author will gladly recifiy this in future editions of this book.

Contents

Introduction

Webster's Dictionary defines an entrepreneur as "one who organizes, manages, and assumes the risks of a business or enterprise."

In the past few decades, entrepreneurs have deservedly earned our attention and respect. They have significantly contributed to our economy and business culture, as well as improved the quality of our lives.

We have come to realize that how they go about their business is equally as important as the business itself. . . maybe even more so. In essence, we can benefit from knowing "what makes them tick."

Like all of us, entrepreneurs are neither perfect nor do they possess all the answers to life's dilemmas. However, they do practice many attributes that are worthy of emulation and adoption by us. Entrepreneurs are willing to put themselves "out there" and to strive for and accomplish their stated mission. They passionately believe in their mission. In mind and spirit, they are confident that the world wants and needs their efforts; they are even convinced that the world will be better for it!

Entrepreneurs find themselves, and often deliberately put themselves, in situations and challenges which demand that they be creative and demonstrate strong leadership in which they have to employ all their knowledge, skills, intuition, articulation, expertise, and character.

Their quests often yield opportunities and growth for other persons they involve in their pursuits.

To succeed, entrepreneurs must display commitment, vision, courage, and confidence. They must be extraordinary leaders, possessing strong character.

The entrepreneurial life is marked by sacrifice, service, and love. It is, then, a full, whole life which is alive and satisfying. Do we all not desire to live with such a sense of accomplishment and peace?

This book attempts to identify and explore the traits, habits, and behaviors that provide a portrait of the entrepreneurial mind and spirit, as well as leadership styles and practices. No assessment can address all the unique nuances of a large group of people, yet the common denominators provide a reliable picture. Likewise, one person cannot, nor should, burden himself to inculcate all of the assets we will explore. The key is to be aware of them and to exercise them as is most fit and helpful.

May I be the first to say that I do not claim to approach being anywhere near to possessing many of the qualities I will enumerate and we will study; but I aim to!

My mission and hope are that through these words, readings, and quotations, you will be informed, inspired, and encouraged to take the most difficult, important step of any journey—the first one!

The impossible is possible! You can do this!

"No retreat, baby, no surrender."[1]

1 Bruce Springsteen from *No Surrender*, 1984

A

"A"
is for
"Attitude"

Attitude

The longer I live, the more I realize the impact of attitude
on life. It is more important than the past, than education,
than money, than circumstances, than failures, than suc-
cesses, than what other people think or say or do. It is more
important than appearance, giftedness or skill. It will make
or break a company . . . a church . . . a home. The remark-
able thing is we have a choice every day regarding the attitude we will embrace for that day. We cannot change our
past . . . we cannot change the fact that people will act in
a certain way. We cannot change the inevitable. The only
thing we can do is play on the one string we have, and that
is our attitude . . . I am convinced that life is 10% what happens to me and 90 percent how I react to it. And so it is with
you . . . we are in charge of our Attitude.
—Chuck Swindoll[2]

This meticulous and concise musing on the topic of attitude
is so astutely word-smithed by Chuck Swindoll that whether
its greater impact would be to begin or end this chapter with it is
indeed a conundrum. For in essence, the decision poetically mir-
rors the very concept of attitude; all relationships and enterprises
begin and end with attitude. As far as life goes it is the Alpha and
the Omega. It is the fuel for the energy that drives all purposeful
initiative. The import and power of attitude cannot be overstated.

In general terms attitude is your perspective, the way you see
and regard things. It is your outlook or point of view, your mind

2 https://www.goodreads.com/quotes/267482-the-longer-i-live-the-more-i-realize-the-impact

set. It colors your affect and all that you say and do. It flavors all your thinking, endeavors, and relationships. It is the fundamental element of your character, being, and personality.

Most people either have a positive or negative attitude. Poet Martin Buxbaum wrote eloquently of this:

> There are two forces working inside of us—one positive and one negative. When the positive is in control, we have confidence in ourselves—we face the world taller and straighter and we have courage. But when the negative side of us takes over, we have doubts and fears, we shrink from problems, we don't enjoy life.
>
> If we realize that we do have two separate and distinct personalities, and that each is constantly seeking control, then we have taken the first step toward a richer, fuller, healthier life. . .
>
> When you find yourself lacking in confidence, you have allowed your negative side to take over, and you should concentrate on your positive side of life. If you don't you are in for trouble, mentally at first, and then physically.

Positive, optimistic, and hopeful people are exuberant about life and exude their enthusiasm to others and their pursuits. They see possibility and opportunity in all things and situations. They relish the journey and firmly trust that there are lessons in every event, even if it has to be learned through sacrifice, strain, and suffering. They are hopeful and confident that all things can lead to transformation and change. Positive people want to be agents of such outcomes and want you to join them!

Zig Ziglar once famously declared: "It is your attitude more than aptitude that determines your altitude." Known for his salesmanship, Ziglar integrates into his thoughts much empirical knowledge that psychologists and researchers have found over the years. A positive can-do attitude is paramount to success in all its various measurable indices. It is, without a close second, the most accurate predictor of success.

During a leadership training program in which I participated as a Boy Scout, a story was told that illustrates Ziglar's theory impactfully. During WW II, a bomber squadron was flying over enemy territory when the lights and controls began to flicker. In response to orders from the pilot, a gunner reported to him that the problem was being caused by a mouse eating the insulation on the wiring but that he could not reach it and stop it. After uttering a quick, "Roger that," the pilot immediately modified the attitude of the wing flaps causing the plane to ascend to a much higher altitude. In what must have seemed like eternity, but was only a few minutes, the flickering ceased. At the higher altitude, with its freezing oxygen-thin air, the mouse succumbed.

Attitude Begets Altitude

In a study of attitude, no voice is more competent and beneficial that that of Dr. Alan Zimmerman, C.S.P, C.P.A.E. He is a devoted student, speaker, and author on this topic as well as others related to personality, skill development, and success. His book *93 Truths* is an enlightening, thorough read.

In expanding on Ziglar's words, Dr. Zimmerman contends that one can change and/or control his or her attitude—the way they feel. Evidence of this fact, Zimmerman explains, can be seen in reflecting on the characteristics of a winner. Most agree that in describing a winner, the following is noted: positive attitude, enthusiasm, determination, motivation, confidence, optimism, dedication, and being happy, kind, hardworking, and patient. None of these qualities has much to do with genetics or physical and mental ability; but they all fall into self-chosen attitudes or behaviors. In essence, you can control whether or not you will be a winner or victor in life—regardless of natural ability, or your nature.

In further development of the winner/loser theory, Zimmerman presents the contrasts between them:

- The winner is always a part of the answer. The loser is always a part of the problem.

- The winner always has a plan. The loser always has an excuse.

- The winner says, *"Let me help you."* The loser says, *"That's not my job."*

- The winner sees an answer for every problem. The loser sees a problem in every answer.

- The winner says, *"It may be difficult, but it's possible."* The loser says, *"It may be possible, but it's too difficult."*

Zimmerman concludes his contrast by emphasizing the attributes of the winner:

- A winner knows that winning involves a lot more than coming out on top . . . or having the highest score or the most delegates.

- A winner sets high goals. You can't be a winner by simply wandering through life and working with no particular end in mind.

- A winner is disciplined. Setting high goals is a waste of time if you are not willing to work hard to achieve them.

- A winner is *highly motivated*. Without a high degree of motivation, you will never make the sacrifices you need to make to achieve the results you want.

You *can* be a winner. You can have a winner's attitude. You really can.

People who enjoy life and who feel successful are positive, productive people who inspire all those they know. They lead with their attitude. Their contentment and satisfaction derive largely from the mindset of their choosing, and the accomplishments they attain because of it. Attitude trumps aptitude, position, status, and power. It is key.

Like many other people, I often fall short of having the attitude and mindset I desire to have. By nature, I lean towards "The glass is half empty" side of the equation. My mother blamed my father's English DNA, and my father was certain it was my mother's Irish DNA!

I have learned that transforming attitude is a matter of will and effort—with the emphasis on effort.

It does not take long into a leadership or business management experience to determine the importance and the impact of attitude. Let me share my story:

My wife and I founded our parent business, Associated Production Services, Inc., on the day after Labor Day, 1977, with seven developmentally disabled adults whom I had developed a relationship with during a four-year tenure of teaching.

Please avail yourself of our brochure at the end of the chapter which gives you a flavor as to our mission and program.

Three months after our founding, we moved from our modified chicken coop to a two-story barn. These quarters were challenging for we worked on the second floor where it was warm, and therefore everything was carried by hand upstairs. We became very adept at the proverbial "bucket brigade" technique!

In May of 1978, we moved again. This time it was to a tire warehouse where we now had two loading docks and were working with thirty people and no stairs. Within a year, our contract demands and expanding census necessitated a move to accommodate our growth and ensure preparation for even further expansion and capabilities.

Late on a Friday afternoon, I went to inspect a stand-alone industrial building, quadruple the size of our current site. It required a three-year lease and a $5,000 deposit. Completely mindful that we had no money, I instructed that a lease should be drawn up and that we would visit again on Monday to sign and square up!

That Sunday morning, I was a guest presenter at an adult Bible school class. Although it was not in my notes, I commented on attitude and faith and that my experience to date had taught me that I must be hopeful, trust in self-fulfilling prophecy and mental-image success. It sounded significantly better than the actual butterflies in my stomach I was having about my financial commitment due the next day. I decided to share the tension I was going through and laid out this "test" of attitude and faith I was engaged in.

The class ended and, as I was exiting the room, in an episode that can only be defined as a providential miracle, a woman, Dorothy Wolfinger, placed a check for $5,000 (that's worth $18,000 today!) into my hand! I accepted this largess with a promise that I considered it a loan, which she dismissed readily with these words: "Repayment is not necessary."

During the course of the next week, I did draw up a memo of

understanding that Dorothy reluctantly signed. Over the next two years our relationship grew, and, in honor of it and my payment of the loan, she presented me with a plaque she had painted. Due to an unfortunate turn of events and loss in her life, Dorothy was in need of the funds just when I was able to pay off the loan.

Four months after signing the lease and moving in, on the second anniversary (Labor Day) of our founding, I was driving to work at my usual early hour with the news radio on. The announcer was speaking of a "major seven alarm fire that destroyed a building in Lower Bucks County." My stomach flipped as I turned the corner and was stopped by a police officer.

"What building burned?" I asked.

"The old storm and screen company," he replied.

"That's me!" I barely exhaled. I knew that the former tenant was a window manufacturer, and our tenancy was so young that people did not relate to our occupation.

"The Fire Marshall will want to see you immediately," I heard as I pulled away.

The next hour was the most intense hour of my life. Every sense has been indelibly marked in my memory. The humidity, the acrid smell of the smoke, and the noise of the bulldozer clawing in the remaining shaky walls will never leave me. I can still see the public adjusters thrusting business cards in my face as they told me they represented my insurance company. . . (they lied). I remember fire fighters commenting, or rather questioning me, on how much we would benefit from this. They made me feel embarrassed and ashamed, sullied; no response I made would satisfy such questions.

All I could seem to process was that either someone didn't want me in business, or I had terrible luck; but either way I was woefully underinsured and ruined, and there was no hope. I wanted to run away and have a pity party.

After a period of time, the secretary of the business next door arrived to work and approached me and offered me a desk and a phone in their building. I made a few calls to inform my wife, lawyer, and a few others I felt needed to know.

I next called my father, certain that he would understand my angst and feel sorry for me. As soon as he answered his phone, I blurted out the despair I was feeling and my certainty that I was entitled to quit and be done with all of this. I was miserable and tired, and my conversation was all about me. Never at a loss for words, I was perplexed that, at the end of my diatribe, he did not offer a response. After an awkward period, he asked, "What is happening now?" As he posed this question, I looked out the window and my attention was drawn to a scene in which my dear friend from college, who had left his teaching job to become our production manager, on this, his first day with us, was talking to a van driver and the ten developmentally disabled workers in the van. The look on all of their fallen faces profoundly impacted me, and it does to this day. I went to answer my father when he said, "Caesar, lead your troops!" and hung up.

A short time later, I was joined by a fellow teacher friend upon whom I again tried my martyr speech. He, too, just listened. When I was done, he simply said, "OK, what do we do first?"

I slowly came to the realization that I needed a "serious" attitude adjustment; my thoughts went like this: "I have to be what I HAVE to be; there is no plan B. I need to be the leader I would want to follow, and that others seem to think I am."

In less than a week we found a space, built work tables, and reopened. We also found out that, although no charges were going to be made, the fire was the work of arsonists. We were in the wrong place at the wrong time; but we would survive and, although I recoiled every time someone said, "This will work out. You will never be the same; you will be stronger and smarter," those words were proved true.

As we rebuilt, I saw the benefits of action and taking charge. Initiative and action are therapeutic, and I learned that "feelings follow actions." If you do the positive things of a motivated leader and discipline yourself to conjure only on positive thoughts and speech, you will thrive and succeed.

Thinking in a desired mindset takes discipline and habit. The thoughts that do not contribute to your ideal mindset are often pervasive. I have found that through the practice of prayer, meditation, and mindfulness, you can foster the presence of your desired thoughts and chasten the influence of your unwanted thoughts.

I suggest three or four times a day, as needed, or by schedule, that you recite and reflect on a Scripture, quotation, axiom, or something you have written that you find grounds you, centers you, and gives you peace.

Below I include some centering words and readings from which you might adopt a saying or mantra. Your goal is to quiet yourself. Let them provide focus for the next period of time. These will inspire you, and, in turn, you will lead and inspire others.

- Be anxious about nothing; be thoughtful about everything.

- Did any of the things I was fearing yesterday happen?

- Do Good and be kind.

- Be the person I want others to see.

- Let go; you have little control.

- Calm.

- This moment; enjoy the process! Perfect!

- Shalom.

- Peace.

- Do a good turn daily.

- Practice compassion.

In the chapter titled *Know Yourself*, we will examine another centering and mind clearing practice—positive affirmation. We will expand our understanding and practice of cogitative, attitude-developing recitations.

I close with an old fable that suggests a great attitude akin to "all things work for good." In other words, be sure to maintain a hopeful and expectant attitude.

Ancient Chinese Proverb

Once upon a time, there was a farmer in the central region of China. He didn't have a lot of money and, instead of a tractor, he used an old horse to plow his field.

One afternoon, while working in the field, the horse dropped dead. Everyone in the village said, "Oh, what a horrible thing to happen." The farmer said simply, "We'll see." He was so at peace and so calm, that everyone in the village got together and, admiring his attitude, gave him a new horse as a gift.

Everyone's reaction now was, "What a lucky man." And the farmer said, "We'll see."

A couple of days later, the new horse jumped a fence and ran away. Everyone in the village shook their heads and said, "What a poor fellow!"

The farmer smiled and said, "We'll see."

Eventually, the horse found his way home, and everyone again said, "What a fortunate man."

The farmer said, "We'll see."

Later in the year, the farmer's young boy went out riding on the horse and fell and broke his leg. Everyone in the village said, "What a shame for the poor boy."

The farmer said, "We'll see."

Two days later, the army came into the village to draft new recruits. When they saw that the farmer's son had a broken leg, they decided not to recruit him.

Everyone said, "What a fortunate young man."

The farmer smiled again, and said, "We'll see."

The moral of the story: There's no use in overreacting to the events and circumstances of our everyday lives. Many times, what looks like a setback may actually be a gift in disguise. And when our hearts are in the right place, all events and circumstances are gifts from which we can learn valuable lessons.

EMPOWERING WORKERS WITH DISABILITIES

IF YOU OR SOMEONE YOU KNOW:

+ Would like to earn a paycheck in a place where people will understand and accommodate disabilities.

+ Are independent with all activities of daily living.

+ Have not been a danger to oneself or others within the last 12 months.

WE OFFER

+ EARN WHILE YOU LEARN

+ PRE-VOCATIONAL TRAINING

+ 5 DAYS A WEEK

+ 5 PENNSYLVANIA LOCATIONS

+ A WORK CENTER THAT WORKS!

+ SUPPORT FOR INDIVIDUAL NEEDS

+ COMMUNITY PARTICIPATION

SINCE 1977

Associated Production Services, Inc. (APS) helps developmentally disabled adults fulfill their vocational goals. APS provides wage earning work to help train adults with disabilities to do labor intensive assembly and packaging jobs.

Our team of dedicated professionals provides services to 550 people at five locations in the north and southeast regions of Pennsylvania.

WE CAN GIVE YOU

+ **DIVERSITY** of people, skills and work experiences

+ **TRAINING** options for individuals in a variety of skills

+ **INNOVATION** to accomodate individual differences and abilities

+ **COMMUNITY** connection through volunteering and skill-building activities

SAFETY AND WELL-BEING

+ Equal opportunity employer

+ Over 40 years of service

+ Licensed by the Department of Human Services

+ Trained and Certified in Community Participation and Employment Supports

B

"B"
is for
"Beg, Borrow, and Barter"

Beg, Borrow, and Barter

1: Beg

Beg may be too strong a word here but the preferred word "Ask" begins with the letter "A" and we have already used "A" for attitude! Being able to ask, or, in other words, request something from people is an essential tool to successful entrepreneurship.

Asking of people often requires nerve and overcoming some awkwardness, but one cannot be an entrepreneur and a leader without making "asks." There will be countless opportunities to present ideas, plans, and requests for all manner of things. . . even money!

At countless times throughout your life and work you will need, or could benefit from, what others possess or have the ability to purvey to you. It may be information or it may be something material. In most instances an "ask" is considered a favor, not a financial transaction. If the ask is for money, you must be prepared with an exact plan in writing as to the terms and conditions you are requesting and how it will be returned.

There are some pointers I would like to offer that I believe will give you confidence and increase the likelihood of a positive response to your "ask":

- Courtesy is vital. "Please" and "thank you" cannot be overused; they move mountains. "Yes, sir" and "Yes, ma'am" are not outdated terms; they immediately express respect and decorum to the party receiving them. They indicate that you are serious about what you intend to accomplish and that you value the person you are addressing.

- Exercise every measure possible to make your "ask" in person. No other medium is as effective and efficient as face to face. Being able to read the initial response, for instance, allows you to amend what is or is not resonating and, therefore, to modify your approach.

- Honoring the appointed hour with promptness is paramount.

- Be prepared. Practice your "ask" beforehand. Strive to present it in a fashion referred to as an "elevator pitch", i.e., thirty to forty seconds. You do not want to appear flustered and rushed but rather very well thought out and respectful of the other person's time. You want your listener to know that you respect him or her as a quick study and very astute.

- Shake hands only if a hand is offered to you upon meeting.

- Begin by expressing your gratitude for the person's willingness to meet and for his or her valuable time.

- As soon as it is possible, offer a compliment. It could be the office, or the company's service to the community, or something else you studied and learned about it.

- If in doubt, overdress for the occasion.

- Never make the conversation about you unless you are asked a specific question. Limit "war stories" and stay focused on the task.

- Always state that you are prepared to offer remuneration if it is needed. This willingness on your part shows your commitment and that you realize and appreciate the value of what you are asking for; it shows that you take care of your dealings. It is surprising how many people want to help ambitious people and contribute to a thoughtful enterprise.

- Be very attentive and react quickly if you sense from your party it is time to go.

- Should you receive an initial "no," offer words of gratitude and thanks anyway, and then ask that if in the future the person you are asking might have an idea or a lead you could act upon, and that you would appreciate their continued interest. Leave them your contact information.

One of my biggest asks came in my second year of teaching. In the summer of 1975, a fellow teacher and I proposed to our supervisor that we wanted to inaugurate a program whereby we would train and employ some of our developmentally disabled students by forming a venture to build and deliver sturdy, framed, wooden garden sheds, each one complete with a window and a shingled roof. Our "ask" was approved despite us being very short on details!

Our biggest hurdle immediately became the matter of where we were going to house our business. We were only going to be in business for eight weeks, so a lease was highly unlikely—not to mention that we had no money!

As I drive, I always make it a habit to safely pay attention to the areas I am traversing. In my travels around this time, I had often noticed a large Quonset-type building in a field behind a local church. It looked tired, but it was secure. I inquired of the church secretary about the history and ownership of the building, thinking it belonged to the church'. She explained that it was the assembly hall of the "Loyal Republication Club" and had not been used in several years. She volunteered that the County Recorder of Deeds, a man named Bill Liebig, might be able to help me. Twenty minutes later, I found myself standing in front of Bill. I told him how I came to be aware of him and briefly outlined a proposed program and asked his advice and counsel as to how we might further explore the possible use of the building. After telling me to wait a moment, he walked into an office off to the side and, upon his return, he placed a set of keys in my hands. "Bring these back when you are finished with your project; and good luck with the toilets!" Bill said. He calmly walked away as I asked about a lease agreement, rent, etc. All he said was "Good-bye." We were in business! You never know unless you ask.

2: Borrow

In our discussion of begging—or asking—we spoke of the traditional definition of borrowing, which is to take and use something for a while and then return it. For the entrepreneurial leader there is an interpretation of the word borrow, which when employed into thinking and a creative, solution-based model of problem solving, can positively contribute to this process. There is very little new under the sun. Others have probably faced the same or similar issue, so let's not reinvent the wheel, but rather "borrow" from former solutions or take advantage of something that already exists and can be used in a different, novel way. This is the concept of repurposing—taking an item or idea that is used for one objective or purpose and employing it for another.

Psychologists call it rigidity of thinking when one fears there is only one use for something. This is termed "functional fixedness." Some people, for instance, think that a screwdriver can only be used to turn a screw in or out. Most of us know, however, that with focus and imaginative thought, you can literally list hundreds of perfectly appropriate and useful tasks that a screwdriver might be engaged to do. It is this open mindset that successful people use to unleash solutions for their problems and challenges.

Allow me to share some practical examples of the values of repurposing. In my first year of teaching vocational education to developmentally disabled high school students, I was challenged with the realities that there was no curriculum and no budget for materials! My mission was to have the students experience work by being actively engaged with tools and materials and making things. I was convinced that, if we could make and market some of our products, we could generate revenue to pay for materials and also offer some financial remuneration to the students in our effort to teach them about work and money.

Unique Planters

One day, after some searching and investigating, I saw an unusual planter in someone's front yard (see the picture at the end of the chapter). I chatted with the homeowner and discovered that he had made it himself. It was an old tire and wheel that had been cut with a saw to create a petal design, inverted so that it bloomed open and then was painted a bright, attractive color. It was not long before we were collecting (free of charge—some people might have paid us to take them away for you cannot put tires in a land-fill!) and making planters like this. We sold, without exaggeration, thousands! Except for the cost of the paint, every sale went to the students. The repurposing of tires provided us with a valuable skill training and business experience and was completely self-funded (see pictures at the end of the chapter).

In very similar fashion, we also decorated discarded wooden pallets with American flag designs or holiday pictures such as a Christmas tree. Where people who purchased these skids hung or placed them was amazing!

The practice of using the repurposing theory became very impactful in the early days of the New York Style Bagel Chip Company, of which I was a founding partner. Our original concept and production model involved purchasing stale bagels from local shops, slicing them with a deli type slicer by hand, spraying oil on both sides with a portable paint sprayer, and then shaking garlic salt on both sides. In less than a day, we realized that manually slicing the bagels was impossible. After twenty minutes, workers were done for the day! Literally within hours the model proved to be a disaster. We needed to address the woefully inefficient and fatiguing manual slicer we were using to cut the bagel into thin slices. Our thinking was that we needed to slice and deposit the chips automatically into an oil sprayer. To design and fabricate such a machine would take many months and be extremely costly. We needed to see if a machine existed that could be repurposed.

After some extensive research, we learned of a company in Blacklick, Ohio, that made machines that slice salami and cheese onto pizza dough or sandwich bread. The product to be sliced is placed into tubes (like rain downspouts) and they then centiliter or cross back and forth over a circular blade. These round band saw blades were long enough to cut up to forty inches across. With the proper coordination of speed of the oven conveyor belt and the number of times that the tubes pass across the blade, you can completely fill the oven with product. When we first contacted the Grote Company, we asked them if they could slice bagels. Their answer was: "Of course we can; what is a bagel?" When we founded the company in 1984, only 7 percent of Americans knew what a bagel was—let alone a bagel chip!

Further visits and conversations led to Grote building a thirty-six-inch-wide slicer that deposited nine slices evenly across the full width of the conveyor belt. From there, they went through a top and bottom oil spraying machine and then a seasoning application unit. . . all this with no hands!

Vegetable Oil

Another repurposing initiative from the bagel chip tenure involved the storage of vegetable oil.

The push of rising sales of the bagel chip was welcome but always stressful to the budget and current capacity. When production must be more robust, everything needs to expand to accommodate it.

In less than a year we went from purchasing five-gallon pails of oil for the chip to fifty-five-gallon drums. The drums were awkward to handle and hard to dispose of when empty. The next step was to receive tanker truck loads but we did not have a tank because they cost about $20,000 at the time. Once again, we engaged some creative repurposing and attended an auction where we bought a used tanker truck. We took the tank off the frame and wheels, and placed it next to our building on a pad with a hose going from the tank to the sprayer. We were now able to store a full load. Budget—$2,600—IN ALL!

The most significant repurposing success I ever achieved also involved the bagel chips. When you take a conventional bagel that is about three inches thick and then cut it into slices, the first and second slices and the second-to-last slices are full size in dimension but are more "half-moon" shaped. These pieces obviously bake more quickly than full slices so sometimes they burn. These pieces are not saleable and they are considered "shrinkage" to your production yield. They are lost money in product and labor.

In the recesses of my memory, I reflected on a baked loaf with orange glaze that I remember was being sold in local bake shops when I was a kid. It had a distinct shape that I determined must have come from a two-piece "clamshell" pan. Research led me to the Ecko-Glaco Baking Pan Company in Chicago. When I described what I remembered as a three-inch diameter, eight-inch-long loaf, the salesman I was speaking with said that I must have a pretty good memory because they had not made those pans in decades! He thought, however, he might have a few in the plant. If he found them, he would send me one. He did find one. After literally weeks of heated discussion with my bagel baking team—who all belabored me with all the reasons you could not bake a bagel dough in a pan—I became frustrated and annoyed and proceeded out to the bakery floor. I placed a lump of dough into the pan, closed it, and sent it through the oven. It baked perfectly! Everyone told me I got lucky, but that it was still not good because it did not have a hole—and a bagel has to have a hole in the middle. I ran to the maintenance shop and grabbed a piece of quarter-inch aluminum rod. I literally shoved it through the middle of a new lump of dough and baked it. After opening the mold and letting the dough cool, the rod was pulled out—leaving a perfect hole.

Each pan produced four loaves. So, we now had a method to bake loaves of bagels which when put into the slicer came out a consistent full-size slice. There was no shrinkage at all. We increased the yield of salable product by 33 percent because now there were no half-moon shaped slices at either end as there are when you slice a typical bagel. Imagine the cost savings and efficiencies! This development was a significant contributor to the economic viability of the business and its attraction to a future buyer. Not being a baker, I would have assumed a loaf pan would never work with a "tenacious" bagel dough, but, this turned out to be my best asset. Sometimes ignorance is bliss! Did I trust the experience and value the opinion of my team? Of course I did, but, even more, I valued verification and the possibilities of being proven wrong!

Another illustrative example of striving to seek "stock" or "off the shelf" currently available products, especially when you are in startup phase and sales are in a "forecast" mode; (i.e., zero), was our efforts to acquire a package for our bagel chips.

Upon researching and getting initial quotes, we learned that the bag we needed was going to have to be quite complex and expensive until we were able to buy millions at a time. The bag needed to be lined with an oil-resistant film so that there were no grease stains; strong enough to resist crumbling of the chip; able to stand on a shelf; and capable of being resealed to keep the product fresh. Printing plates and dies alone where thousands of dollars—and payable in advance.

As Steve Jobs once famously encouraged, we needed to "use our environment." We needed to call others whom we thought could help us and think about our historical experiences for solutions.

As we engaged in this process, we were musing and brainstorming when we touched on the fact that if we could find a bag that holds water, we would be well on our way. A paper bag that holds water seemed impossible, but it was the idea spark we needed.

This discussion led me to reflect on a recent memory. I took my first flight at age thirty two and, as with many first-time fliers, I was anxious and I remember being both relieved and intrigued when I located and examined the "barf bag" discreetly housed in the seat pocket in front of me. Yes. . . . We did! We contacted the manufacturer of barf bags and bought several cases. We then bought an inexpensive single-color label-printing machine and we were in business! They were perfect and satisfied every requirement we had to have.

As the business and volume warranted, we evolved into pre-printing our bags with the same structure and the exact dimensions of our original "barf bag".

I know this is not very appetizing, but after selling millions of bags' worth of product, I can confidently say I am not aware of any time when someone commented about the other primary use of our packaging!

Digital Scales

My final example of integrating existing products and technologies into your creative problem solving involves digital scales. Almost every developmentally disabled person I train cannot reliably count. Being in the contract packaging business, where literally everything is packed to a specific count, this is a serious obstacle. Historically, we would, for example, when packaging twenty-five screws into a box, draw twenty-five lines on a piece of paper and have the worker place a screw on each line and then scoop them up into the box. One day I was observing a sandwich being made at our local deli. I saw the slices of ham being placed on this scale that weighed digitally to 1/100 of a pound. I was amazed with the speed and accuracy. I had a Nirvana moment. I borrowed from the bank the highest amount of money I had ever borrowed, and bought a

Hobart digital scale. Today they cost virtually nothing! I then commissioned an electrical engineer to set up a system whereby when the scale reached a desired weight, a red light would go on and a buzzer would sound. Our workers would place the box on this scale and fill it until the light came on and the buzzer sounded. They did not even have to identify the numbers on the scale. Imagine the time they saved! We could, without exaggeration, do seven to ten times the volume with the same number of people. The use of what became dozens of scales propelled our business because it increased our capacity to serve and our quality was perfect. Thank goodness for that ham sandwich!

I must go a few layers deeper in our discussion of the digital scale.

Our company, Associated Production Services, Inc. (APS), is a Pennsylvania Department of Health and Human Services certified Vocational Training Facility and work center. We currently train 500 developmentally disabled adults in six locations along the eastern border of Pennsylvania.

Our mission is to prepare our trainees to one day secure a position in the community in "competitive employment." We utilize, for our training, the work environment that is created by being a contract packaging business that provides high-volume packaging services to all manner of companies. The greatest portion of work we do is for the confectionary industry, packaging their pre-wrapped product. We also do traditional assembly work of metal and plastic consumer goods.

Through their involvement in these tasks, our trainees develop the motor skills, work habits, attitudes, and ability to cooperate with peers and management. It is then a "living classroom."

Work centers such as ours have a special license issued by the U.S. Department of Labor that permits us to remunerate our trainees for their wage-earning efforts with a piece rate pay, as opposed to a guaranteed hourly rate of pay. This license is only issued to us after strict compliance to regulations and documentation that ensures a just and fair system of compensation. It is a win-win program. It is crucial for our economic viability, for the challenges that our people work through often results in less production output than a "typical" employee can provide. This program ensures that all parties benefit and the employment of developmentally disabled people can take place.

As you can easily deduce, being paid by the piece means that if management can in any way increase the speed of output (i.e., the number of finished components), then this is most welcomed and appreciated by our disabled trainees. With efficiency comes more compensation. It is all about efficient motion, proper job setup, and processes.

When we are able to introduce mechanical adaptations to complement and satisfy the cognitive and motoric challenges our people have, such as in using a digital scale, to count it is a win-win outcome.

Every day, in every way our staff aid our trainees to perform and achieve to their highest potential. We borrow the practices, technologies, and wisdom and disciplines of other people, and then use them to our benefit. We "network" on a big scale (no pun intended)!

A Final Musing

When I was in junior high school, struggling academically, my best friend and I took an introductory course in graphic arts (printing) within the industrial arts department. I thoroughly absorbed the experience and did well, even though I am not generally facile with tools.

Near the end of high school, dreaming I might own my own establishment some day I decided that I would pursue a career in printing. My financial situation limited my college options to one of the New Jersey State colleges that offered printing. By some miracle I was accepted into Trenton State College (now the College of New Jersey). Upon arrival I was immediately sobered with the reality that graphic arts were integrated into the curriculum that trained and certified industrial arts teachers—all of whom were skilled with tools and were craftspeople!

Although I initially decided to transfer out and attend a printing school in New York City, I held back—thank goodness.

I gradually found my niche and was very fortunate to have professors who appreciated and recognized attitude and effort to be equal to acumen and artistry.

Although I never appreciated it at the time, I was exposed to classes that dealt with the fundamental precepts of manufacturing and mass production. I learned about manufacturing tools and tooling, materials, technologies, methods to achieve quality interchangeable parts, efficiency of motion, assembly line strategies, and time-and-motion methods and programs.

Harboring a desire to work with the developmentally disabled, and knowing I would never be a competent shop teacher, I found myself drawn to the idea of teaching vocational education to special-needs students. I applied for, and received, a scholarship for a Master's Degree in Special Education which I completed in one year.

The rest, as they say, is history! I taught for a brief period and then, encouraged by parents of my students, social workers, and peers, my wife and I resigned our positions and started APS as a not-for-profit company in July of 1977.

Fundamentally, APS's entire mission, concept, and model is based on the borrowed body of knowledge I learned in my industrial arts and technology training and classes. This knowledge provided the foundation to, at a minimum, have an idea as to whom to seek out and where to go to borrow the knowledge, expertise, experience, techniques, tools, or methods I needed to serve my trainees and grow my business. The Gestalt of these borrowings allowed me to succeed at purveying vocational training opportunities and work for those entrusted to me. I was then able to serve them by having them learn tasks, develop speed and perseverance, earn money, and enjoy success and the feeling of dignity a job establishes.

3: Barter

Bartering is the technique or system whereby parties exchange goods or services for other goods or services without using money. In other words, you trade after assessing the parity of the value of what is being exchanged.

It is in age-old practice and can be especially productive between parties with limited cash funds.

A few years ago, the History Channel aired a show called "Down

East Dickerin." It is a clever exposé of "Mainers" who make a living bartering in creative and convoluted ways. It is illuminating to see how skills, knowledge of trades, and / or goods can be used as leverage to acquire other goods that can then be sold or further bartered after they are repaired or improved.

A few years into our business, I realized that depending exclusively on subcontract work being procured from customers was unwise. Ideally, we needed to supplement outside work with in-house initiatives of producing our own products. This would allow us to be masters of our own destiny and assure consistent production and cash flow. I had some experience trying to market and distribute various products and I quickly learned that it is a time-consuming, separate venture altogether.

While attending a Bible study group, I developed a friendship with an older gentleman who was proprietor of a cookie baking company that specialized in "giant" five-inches-in-diameter cookies that he purveyed to schools during school days and to swim clubs in the summer. I had heard that he was not content with his business model as it was very labor intensive so his presence was needed in the bakery almost full-time and thus his marketing efforts were suffering. As "labor" is my business, I asked him if we could visit and brainstorm on a potential win-win joint venture of some design. Our discussions quickly led to a zero acquisition of the company and its assets in exchange for an exclusive distribution agreement with the owner. In essence, we bartered with each other for our mutual benefit.

The relationship and business went very well for several years. We were able to engineer the baking process so that developmentally disabled people did all the baking and packaging. Unfortunately, the cookie market became enamored with a style of cookie called "soft batch." Our cookies were hockey pucks in five days! The process of making soft batch was expensive and beyond our financial capabilities, so we needed to move on.

At just this time we became partners in the bagel chip business largely because of the success we had in baking, so this bartered alliance was huge for us.

C

"C"
is for
"Communication"

Communication

Communication is the lifeblood of all interpersonal relationships. It is key to effective and efficient outcomes in every facet of our lives and enterprise.

The ability to organize and articulate with conviction ensures for successful achievement of the goals and plans we are discussing and enables us to infuse our spirit and personality into our ventures and inspire those who are involved with us.

Good leadership and skilled communication are mutually dependent on each other.

The dictionary tells us that "communication is the imparting or exchanging of information or news."

Generally, there is an encoder, or sender, who issues content; and there is a decoder, or recipient, who receives the message. When the two share the same content, communication has been established. There is a shared responsibility for meaning.

Many times, when communicating as a leader, parent, or manager, the content of our message includes an expected or requested action in the carrying out of a dictate or order. I greatly respect, and often employ, the military protocol for such communication. Upon the completion by the sender, the recipient replies "Roger, Wilco." The "Roger" confirms that communication has taken place. It is understood that the "Wilco" is short for "will comply"—in other words, "I understand and I will do it!"

George Bernard Shaw stated, "The single biggest problem with communication is in the illusion it has taken place."

In our general discourse and dialog, we must be mindful that most people retain 20 percent of the content they hear. It is critical, therefore, especially in business, that documentation be prepared whenever possible to verify the occurrence, and summarize the content of all communication that has been engaged in. This documentation memorializes the content and can be further utilized as reminders, follow-up action points, or when clarification is required.

Listening

Someone once quipped, "God gave us two ears but only one mouth." Some people say that's because He wanted us to spend twice as much time listening as talking. Others claim it's because He knew that listening was twice as hard!

Most of us are very able hearers, but we do not readily listen—listening is that act of focused intention and attention to what is being expressed. Successful communication is greatly enhanced when one chooses to demonstrate and practice active listening. By doing so, the listener creates a positive emote of calm, an observable desire to know and understand, which shows respect and a willingness to reach consensus. Listening inherently sets the platform for reciprocal attention to be given as the listener has time to be afforded equal time to offer and speak his or her thoughts. The mutual benefits are more than worth it to each party in turn.

Finally, by listening, the hearer can often determine the real issues and configure ideas and solutions that have focus and clarity. He, or she, can better read body language, formulate questions that probe for data, history, opinions, and ideas and so on.

By listening purposefully, you cultivate in your speaker a feeling that you sincerely want to understand and that you are reasonable and thoughtful. Listening should not be appearing to be waiting to talk. When someone begins to talk and the person listening immediately interrupts, it is rude, disrupting, and colors any further discourse in a counterproductive, negative way.

Active, purposeful listening should ultimately lead to a complete understanding of what another person has said. You can audit this by giving feedback of your takeaways. Do this by clarifying and summarizing. Questions might include, "So what you're saying is. . ." "So, what you need is. . ." or "So, in summary, what we've agreed to do is. . ."

A final note on communication regards timing and place. I think it is a positive start, and helpful, when you phone, text, or bump into someone, that you begin by asking how he or she is doing and whether this would be a good time to spend with you. If you know it is going to be more than five minutes, giving the estimated time you anticipate is a must. Obviously, if your party cannot accommodate, you must set a time that works for you both.

Your attitude and affect from approach to saying goodbye is fundamental in communication. A calm, quiet voice and demeanor cultivates a receptive listener. Courtesy is a must. It establishes a platform of civility that contributes to the mutual respect and trust that ensures both parties feel valued and acknowledged.

To conclude, communication is the foundation for the development of trust and honesty which, when established, assures for success and achievement. Trust is the grease that oils the gears of collaboration, consensus, and confidence. It may seem a bit harsh but here is a good starting point: "Say what you mean, and mean what you say."

The following pieces mostly confirm and repeat our understandings, but their perspectives might be worthy of your review.

The sources for the first two works are noted. I do not recall how or where I found the one titled "Effective Communication Skills." The last two are interoffice memos I authored.

In 1981 Ken Blanchard and Spencer Johnson wrote their now classic book entitled *The One Minute Manager— Enjoy More Success with Less Stress*. It is an efficient and very practical piece.

This book might just as well have contributed to the chapter on Leadership. It is that helpful and applicable to so many situations and challenges faced by managers of all stripes.

Blanchard and Johnson's work concisely reveals three secrets that are, in my opinion, jewels: One Minute Goals, One Minute Praisings, and One Minute Reprimands. By the conclusion of the book I assure you that you will want, and be able, to apply them. Their counsel is very effective as well as being timesaving.

One-Minute Goal Setting is Simply:

1. Agree on your goals.

2. See what good behavior looks like

3. Write out each of your goals on a single sheet of paper using less than 250 words.

4. Read and re-read each goal, which requires only a minute or so each time you do it.

5. Take a minute once in a while out of your day to look at your performance, and

6. See whether or not your behavior matched your goal.

One-Minute Praising works well when you:

1. Tell people up front that you are going to let them know how they are doing.

2. Praise people immediately.

3. Tell people what they did right—be specific.

4. Tell people how good you feel about what they did right, and how it helps the organization and the other people who work there.

5. Stop for a moment of silence to let them *"feel"* how good you feel.

6. Encourage them to do more of the same

7. Shake hands or touch people in a way that makes it clear that you support their success in the organization.

I benefited substantially studying and utilizing One Minute Reprimands. This is an area of supervision that has always been a stress point for me. I quote from the book:

The One Minute Reprimand works well when:

1. Tell people beforehand that you are going to let them know how they are doing and in no uncertain terms.

The first half of the reprimand:

2. Reprimand people immediately.

3. Tell people what they did wrong—be specific.

4. Tell people how you feel about what they did wrong—and in no uncertain terms.

5. Stop for a few seconds of uncomfortable silence to let them *feel* how you feel.

The second half of the reprimand:

6. Shake hands, or touch them in a way that lets them know you are honestly on their side.

7. Remind them how much you value them.

8. Reaffirm that you think well of them but not of their performance in this situation.

9. Realize that when the reprimand is over, it's over.

Effective Communication Skills

Communication skills are absolutely critical for success in life. Sometimes we encounter individuals with whom we disagree or encounter new issues which are unfamiliar to us. This could be particularly true in academics. We also encounter problems which must be resolved. It is important, in order to maximize our own understanding, to approach these issues in an open and positive way. The following USAA guidelines provide a basis for effectively communicating with others.

- Identify the issue

- Many times conversations blur because the people who are talking address separate issues. You need to identify what, exactly, you're discussing. For example, is the issue staying out late or is it the need for freedom? Though the two issues may be related, perhaps you can reach a compromise that addresses everybody's needs.

- Focus on the issue

- Family disputes sometimes begin about one thing and end up about everything else. No doubt actions and activities are related, but it is hard to resolve the accumulated difficulties of personal relationships all at once. Most bridges are built a little at a time.

- Attack the issue and not the person

- Sometimes, people assume that the reason for a disagreement is that the other person is just hardheaded, immature, or something similar. Saying so only makes the person you disagree with defensive and more likely to think the same thing about you.

- Listen with an open mind

- When most of us anticipate arguments, we envision winning them, or at least making our own points decisively. *But the key to resolving disputes is listening to the other person.* This is how you find points of agreement and places where you can compromise. If you do not listen with an open mind, you may hastily reject a solution that is best for everybody.

- Treat the other person's feelings with respect

- This is an important consideration in any argument, but particularly in family discussions where emotions are likely to be high. People who care about the person they are talking to have an especially strong need to believe that their feelings are being considered.

From the Desk of J. Jay Belding

July 12, 2013

Staff,

During our recent self-evaluations, over half of you expressed concerns about *communication*. Please allow me to express some thoughts and, I hope, some practical suggestions:

When you have information—Ask yourself who else might benefit from also knowing it. Take the time to share it.

- Try to use texting or email if possible. Writing provides documentation and clarity.

- When "nextelling" or phoning, begin by asking if this is a good time, state how long you think the conversation will take, and identify the subject matter. Respect a polite "Now is not a good time" answer and establish when it would be a good time to have this conversation.

The above suggestions should also be followed when impromptu meetings occur, i.e., you run into someone in passing.

One form of communication with management is to use the suggestion box on our website, www.apspackage.com. This is a confidential way to inform management of issues or concerns.

Attitude

Nothing enhances a conversation like friendliness and politeness. No in-service or training is going to develop a respectful tone; it must come from within.

Let's all strive to honor each other by respecting each other's time and by being attentive listeners to direct and well-thought-out communication.

From the Desk of J. Jay Belding

July 26, 2013

. . . more on Communication, especially when a disagreement has occurred.

"First to understand, second to be understood."
When respectfully approached by someone to have a conversation and assuming it is a good time for both parties, try first and foremost to be an *active* listener. Make your first response something like "This is what I hear you saying." This will enable you to audit the intent and content of what you have heard.

Through engaged listening, you find points of agreement and places where you can compromise. Clearly establish those points you agree on, then seek solutions to those areas you do not.

"Speak with honesty and candor—avoid war stories."
Be forthright and direct in your conversation. This shows your respect for the others' time commitments. Stay on task. Do not let the conversation drift into other areas not related to the topic at hand.

"Perfection is the enemy of progress."
Any resolve that addresses 80 percent to 90 percent of an issue with 20 percent effort is a worthy goal. One can build on this success. After reaching resolve and agreement, acknowledge closure on these decisions.

"Praise in public, criticize in private."
Any conversation which might include a constructive criticism should be held in private, and any time praise is offered it should be shared with others if at all possible.

D

"D"
is for
"Delegating and Delegatees"

Delegating and Delegatees

Delegating is sometimes difficult for competent, strong-minded leaders. Their skill sets and ego often lead to a mindset that they can do it all—that it is "easier to do it myself." This rationalization not only prohibits efficiency but more importantly stymies the growth of your team members and then the organization as a whole.

Effective leaders must put aside EGO (*E*dging *G*rowth *O*ut) and accept the notion that their responsibilities and tasks are to boost the engagement levels of those who work alongside them.

At its core, delegating requires humility. You must concede and accept that you cannot "do it all" and acknowledge that others can do as well as you or even better than you! You need, as a delegator, to embody the precept of an old adage, "None of us is as skilled as all of us."

By delegating, you nurture the growth of the delegatees, and, in due course, the entire organization. The feelings of affirmation and trust people receive by being delegated to brings great satisfaction and a sense of belonging. The assignment itself gives purpose and builds the confidence of the one tasked. The act of delegating creates in the delegatee a confidence in his or her value and role with the enterprise and its mission.

To develop the practical side of delegation, I offer two works at the end of the chapter which I have utilized over the years. The first notes, entitled "Five Steps to Attentive Delegation," were disseminated during a training seminar I attended conducted by Jack Dueck of People Management Associated in Grantsville, Maryland. The second work is from an article found in the Managing People newsletter/magazine. Together, I believe they provide a thorough, practical outline.

The one additional comment I would make is that I believe it is crucial, when assigning a task, to provide what I call the "accuracy percentage." In other words, share the level of the depth of where you need to be in order to utilize the information you are seeking. Many times, you only need 90 percent accuracy which could be achieved in a few minutes, whereas, to the "penny," or 100 percent, might take a day or two. The sharing of these desired parameters is very helpful to the one tasked with researching the data and specifics.

I find that when I lack the desire or motivation to take on a task it is usually one in which I do not feel proficient and lack confidence. For instance, I am not skilled with power tools, so despite my thoughts that I can get jobs done that require them, I just procrastinate and feel worse! I would be wise to just, from the get-go, acknowledge my innate trepidation and simply retain a skilled craftsman to do the job. Progress should not be delayed by my inability to accept and integrate into my decisions the realities of my strengths and weaknesses. I need to be honest with myself. The moral of the story: "Do not procrastinate; delegate!"

Six Steps to Effective Delegating

Too many managers hold on too tightly—and for too long—to work that someone else could do just as well, possibly better.

1. Explain the purpose of the assignment. Tell people what you hope to accomplish. People who feel they are being brought into the big picture are willing to give it their best. Research has shown that one of the strongest "demotivators" is the lack of explanation or instruction.

2. Be up-front with deadlines. Tell people the real deadline. Even if a person has a reputation for being chronically late, you will earn far more respect by your honesty than by lying about an early deadline.

3. Name all the players. Be sure to tell each person who else is involved in the task. Take the time to explain, for instance,

that once he or she finishes, it will have to go through two other people who will do thus and so to it. Your explanation may forestall deadline problems. Explain, too, who the person can turn to for help if you are not available.

4. Tell the person why you chose him or her for the job. Example: "You're the best writer. Any chance you can get this done today?" This kind of request will make a person want to do a good job, because he or she has been singled out for positive attention.

5. Share the credit. If you constantly steal everyone's thunder, no one will want to work on your assignments. And if an assignment turns out so badly that you wouldn't want credit for it, be careful about how you give criticism. Don't try to knock down egos; give useful information about how the person could do better next time.

6. Share the risk. One of my clients had problems with people who constantly turned in sloppy and inaccurate work. After careful analysis, it became clear that he was following their work so closely that they didn't bother to complete it. They knew he would catch any errors. After he learned how to delegate risk by not double-checking work, the problem disappeared. The people finally felt he was beginning to trust them. Once they had final responsibility for their assignments, they knocked themselves out to do a good job, since their reputations were on the line.

Employees/Delegatees

Leaders need followers. They need to recruit and retain others to join them in their vision and its mission. They need some people to provide focused time and talent and others to provide contracted professional services and consultation. To obtain these human resources, leaders need to be articulate, magnetic, persuasive, and to establish trust. In essence, they need to sell themselves and their enterprise.

People who offer their time and talent for hire do so as employees, remunerated with a salary. To be successful, employers must surround themselves with skilled persons who are energetic, enthused, and totally engaged. Employees need to have a strong sense that they see for themselves an opportunity to contribute, feel valued, and flourish in an organization. In other words, employees do best when they are enriched both financially and spiritually, experiencing joy and fulfillment. Employees want to be part of an effort and to work for leaders they believe in.

Entrepreneurial leaders need to gather people of likeminded morals and ethics yet they must also embrace the need to be diligent in seeking to create a diverse group in an effort to create a culture of creativity, possibility, and mutual respect among all parties. Diverse perspectives and ideas feed growth.

In the book *Good to Great*, Jim Collins writes: "To build a successful organization and team you must get the right people on the bus." He claims that great companies and organizations not only follow this bus but also put people in the right seats on the bus!

The unique challenge with a startup venture, usually with cash flow challenges, is to gather the group of employees you need to start a business. Oftentimes, the founders borrow on their personal collateral or create other cash-preserving pursuits such as bartering or offering people ownership in the company in return for either consulting services or agreeing to initially pay less than an employee is worth and who will accept deferred remuneration.

Matthew York, an editor on Viewfinder, in the July 2014 issue captured the early fledgling days best when he said: "So early employees are doing two and three jobs, working long hours, jumping from one urgent matter to another crisis all day and into the evening. Early-stage companies will change, pivot, and serpentine so many times that it confuses even the nimblest team members. If the early staff is not resilient to the multiple interactions of the fledgling enterprise, the venture is bound to fail."

Starting with the leader of the startup, each person must exhibit courage, compassion, and confidence. . . especially when feeling none of them! At all times, expressions of appreciation and encouragement need to be seen and said. The leader and each member of the team must inspire each other as together they aspire to flourish, succeed, and serve.

E

"E"
is for
"Excellence vs. Perfection"

Excellence vs. Perfection

"Striving for excellence motivates you; striving for perfection is demoralizing."
—Harriet Braiker

"Perfect is the enemy of good."
—Voltaire, 1770

"Perfect is the enemy of progress. . . profitability. . . success."
—Many people!

Excellence and perfection are polar opposites of the same attitude. They are the antithesis of each other. Understanding this is vital if you are to measure and identify which one you are engaging in; then, through discernment, to exercise the discipline to eliminate perfectionism.

I have repeatedly observed that many entrepreneurs and like-minded leaders feel compelled to be perfect. Many of us carry this baggage. The dynamics that lead to this proclivity are broad and complex. It is a true nature-versus-nurture dynamic and everything in between! It is a heavy burden. At its worst, perfectionism is a debilitating disease—quite literally.

My study and thinking on this topic has been largely developed through the writings of Marc Winn. On February 27, 2013, he authored a seminal piece entitled, "Perfection-vs-Excellence" on his website.

Marc passionately presents his thoughts and minces no words!

I do not think this topic can be more compassionately addressed, so I quote verbatim.

Are you a perfectionist?
Or do you strive for excellence?

If you think these are the same thing, I'm afraid you're mistaken. They may be related, but they are the opposite sides of the same coin. In fact, they are so antagonistic towards one another that the best way to achieve excellence is by not demanding perfection. So, let's understand the big differences between the two.

Perfectionism is focused on "doing the thing 'right'", how things APPEAR, and if OTHERS think it's done right.

Excellence is about "doing the right thing". It is focused on the REASON for a task, and the RESULTS for it to be a success.

Perfectionism is a thief of time, draining your energy like a blood-sucking vampire. It bullies and criticizes you, and demands unachievable outcomes—since whatever you do is never good enough. It makes you try to live up to some illusion that doesn't exist. Perfection is always out of reach.

The pursuit of excellence keeps you focused on what matters, fills you with energy and can act as your cheerleader. There is no damage to self-esteem, like that found in perfectionism. Perfectionism diminishes your productivity, your efficiency and effectiveness, and worse still, damages your peace of heart and mind. On the other side, productivity is built into the pursuit of excellence.

Often perfectionists will not complete things, not start things, or not even take things on at all, for fear of not being able to do it perfectly. Perfectionism often causes procrastination. Fear of being unable to deliver to some unachievable standard often causes them to completely avoid doing what needs to be done. Perfectionists are terrified of making a mistake, and consequently find themselves stressed, anxious, and desperately focused on not failing. They maintain unrealistic expectations of themselves and of others and will often micromanage, causing undue stress on themselves and others.

Excellence focuses your attention on what's right and working well, rather than what's not working—and this keeps your attention on the positives and how things could be even better. Excellence is limitless and progressive, since you can always reach for greater and greater excellence. Whereas perfection can never be achieved.

Success is really based on taking the right action and getting the feedback to improve and not on getting things totally right every time.

One example of excellence in action is the popular business-building methodology of Lean Startup—which takes a quick, cheap and simple trial-and-error approach without wasting time or resources. This provides consumer feedback and other great benefits during the product development phase, so that startups have a better chance of success without requiring high levels of funding, complex business plans, or the perfect final product.

Develop active excellence by using the Pareto Principle. (Live the 80/20 Rule) When you know that 20 percent of your effort produces 80 percent of your results, this liberates you to focus on each 20 percent that makes the difference. But take this further! If it took you 1 hour to do 1 thing "perfectly", in that 1 hour, you could get 5 things done to 80 percent of perfection. Achieving 5 things to an excellent level will lead to greater success than doing 1 thing perfectly. Take dynamic action for excellence, rather than painstaking inaction for perfection. Embrace what's "good enough" to succeed!

Understand the damage that perfectionism does, and the benefits of aiming for excellence, then ask yourself where perfectionism has taken hold in your life or business. It might be a trait of yourself, a partner, a child, or an employee. Deal with it at all levels, and nurture an ethos of excellence instead. Accept that nobody's perfect. Accept that excellence is a process and a direction, rather than an end point.

There's no fear attached to excellence; anyone can do it,

and it's realistic. To achieve the success you want in all aspects of your life, I invite you to focus on excellence. This way, your results will always be great—and you can always aim for even better!

So remember—you don't have to always do things right—as long as you always do the right thing. Life is much more rewarding and enjoyable this way![3]

Because of the propensity for leaders to seek perfection and its powerful impact, I want to introduce you to three other insightful readings you might want to consider for your additional thinking.

- In an article she offered for *Intouch Magazine*, Christian author Michelle Van Loon examined perfectionism and its impact on faith and life. Here is a taste of her wisdom: "Perfectionism can lead to straight A's, fabulous performances, Instagram-ready looks and lifestyles, and gold medals. But its achievements are rooted in the acid soil of fear and can't produce life-giving fruit" . . . "excellence emerges as a by-product in our lives. The elusive prize of perfectionism isn't our goal. Completion is."

- Neil Patel, entrepreneur and online marketing expert, on August 31, 2015, wrote a piece in *Entrepreneur Magazine* entitled "Your Secret Mental Weapon. Don't Let the Perfect Be the Enemy of Good." I appreciate his take when he says, "Business success is not born from tactics. It is born from those subtle, below the surface mental shifts. And shifts take time."

- A final reading I recommend is from Tracy Brower. Tracy is candid in warning that "perfectionism is predictive of depression." Her advice is this: "Plan for evolution. Have a mindset where improvement is the norm. Learn to discern the elements of a solution that are show-stoppers, and should delay progress to those right versus those that can be launched to test, learn and improve."[4]

3   https://theviewinside.me/perfectionism-vs-excellence/#:~:text=Perfectionism%20is%20focused%20on%20%E2%80%9Cdoing,it%20to%20be%20a%20success.

4   https://www.forbes.com/sites/tracybrower/2020/02/02/perfection-versus-excellence-4-ways-to-ensure-perfection-doesnt-prevent-progress/?sh=5f1a9ca053ef

I summarize by reflecting on a quote from Charles Stanley, a pastor. He mused: "Unhealthy attitudes, perfectionism, false guilt and apathy all undermine our enjoyment of life."

I encourage you to valiantly try to be aware of when you slip into unhealthy attitudes; especially perfectionism. It is self-centered and destructive to your success. Those you lead are impacted by these unhealthy attitudes. Even as fear and anxieties emerge, remind yourself that no one is perfect. In fact, we are all imperfectly perfect! Monitor yourself and change the narrative in your mind—one thought at a time. In due course, you will create positive mindful habits and your words and actions will be the proof.

Maybe the Cub Scouts have it right. Their motto: "Do your best!"

F

"F"

is for

"Fortitude"

Fortitude

The root word "fort" says it all—strength. The purposes, passion, and plans of the entrepreneurial thinking leader all necessitate the engagement of a singular focus and fortitude. Focus describes your central intent or activity. It is your passion, your vocation or "call," the thing you know you are meant and built to do. Fortitude is the mental and emotional strength used when facing difficulty, adversity, danger, or temptation encountered while in pursuit of your focus and vision.

No one has the DNA to employ and integrate these lofty necessities for success; but, with intention and sacrifice, through practice, routine, and, in time, habit, they are achievable.

The person who desires to strive, attain, achieve, and perform well is an inspiration to all and worthy of emulation and imitation. The parallels between the pursuit of physical strength and prowess, and the development of cognitive and mental strength are striking in their similarity. To achieve in either domain, the will, determination, and process to achieve are coincident.

Discipline is a must for achievement. It is defined as a system of rules and conduct.

Further reflection would add to this definition as it being a mindful intent to engage yourself in that which you planned or intended to do. Often, for example, when you go to the gym to work out, it requires you to will yourself to do exactly what you do not want to! Discipline is overcoming excuses. It is a deliberate intent to leave comfort and complacency and make yourself expend effort to become even, at times, uncomfortable doing so. Diligence, then, is careful and persistent work or effort you put forth as a result of your discipline. Once you have engaged discipline and diligence, persistence becomes a vital requirement. It is being firm, resolute, and showing obstinate continuance in a course of action in spite of difficulties and/or opposition. Winston Churchill moved a kingdom when he said, "Never give in; never give in; never give in." Many others have echoed this sentiment—the Bible speaks of how a righteous man may fall down seven times and yet stand up the eighth time (see Proverbs 24:16).

Perseverance is the cousin of persistence! Perseverance is the ongoing "failure is not an option" attitude and source for ongoing action. It is remaining steadfast, unshakable, and immovable. It is therefore a marathon of energy and enterprise. "When the going gets tough; the tough get going" becomes your mantra. It is the commitment of your will to never quit. "Quitters never win; and winners never quit."

Finally, tenacity is another cousin of persistence. Of immeasurable impact on my life and business was a relationship I had with a couple whom we partnered with to form the New York Bagel Chip Company. Their disciplined attention to detail and their tenacity led to our success. Their commitment to excellence and sheer will was a model to me and all those who worked for us. I remember vividly that at my first visit to their office I saw a sign on the desk that stated, "Tenacity beats brain and brawn." Tenacity is holding fast; it is hyper persistence, and very impactful.

When perseverance and tenacity are needed, it is often to address a challenge or a road block—or even a potential failure. These events demand the influence of applied enterprise. To be enterprising is having and showing initiative and being able to engage in resourcefulness. Resourcefulness is the act of thinking critically in seeking a solution to an obstructing or interfering incident or situation. It is incumbent upon leaders to find within themselves or seek out others who can craft creative and efficient ways to solve and overcome these disturbing issues.

This discussion of commitment to purpose and having the strength to forge ahead is not complete without reflecting on determination.

Determination is having a strong feeling that you are going to embark on something that you will not allow anyone or anything to stop. You have no uncertainty and you are resolute. You are therefore admirably purposeful, stalwart, and unwavering. These attributes are often necessary and need to be called upon following a decision or determining a path or plan of action. You must strive to be sure and confident, moving forward with conviction. "Trust your stuff," as baseball pitchers say to themselves. Or to quote John F. Kennedy, "We must go forth with vim and vigor."

A very helpful illustrative read on this subject would be the book *Deliberate Discomfort: How U.S. Special Operations Forces Overcome Fear and Dare to Win by Getting Comfortable Being Uncomfortable*, by Jason B.A. Van Camp and Andy Symonds.

The summation, here, is that it takes the willful application of diligence, determination, and discipline to build your strengths. In the end, intrinsic motivation is the key to success. The beauty of this is that if we exercise these traits, we not only achieve our goals, but we also build a platform of competency and good habits that become a part of our character which we can employ in every facet of our lives, especially our leadership. Achievement becomes addictive and allows you to feel whole and alive. It is contagious!

One model that has worked well for me to stay motivated and strong is to involve others in my journey. These intimate friends or colleagues are trusted to have my best interests in their heart. They pledge to be honest and forthright. Each of us commits to hold the other accountable to "show up and work hard," and to answer to each other if we have failed or neglected to reach our stated goals. Needless to say, the introduction of some friendly goading and competition is just an added bonus and a welcome distraction!

G

"G"

is for

"The Golden Rule"

The Golden Rule

How to Treat Others

I appreciate the message and its creative presentation every time I see the poster or bumper sticker with the motif COEXIST:

I am often flooded with the thought of how peaceful and wonderful life would be if we could achieve this axiom in the world. But I also muse as to whether to just exist is really living? Surely, there must be a tenet, that if we all practiced and adhered to, we could universally and equally enjoy all the benefits on earth and in our lives.

All leaders have to choose their relational style. I look to the entrepreneurial traits that I often have witnessed. My experience is that most successful leaders and managers ultimately settle on using the Golden Rule as their fundamental platform for how they will relate to people they encounter in all their pursuits.

The Golden Rule, spoken by Jesus, states: "In everything do to others what you would have them do to you."

The Golden Rule defines an ethical conduct. It is the guiding principle of treating others as you want to be treated. It is so beautiful in its wholeness. It completely negates reciprocity and leaves no ambiguity or "situational ethics" analysis. It truly is the unequivocal core value that can ensure flourishing relationships. I would propose all people to use it. It is a code we could all live by, and, in so doing, lose nothing and gain everything.

The Golden Rule is antithetical to much of what our culture propagates. Practicing it requires one to be humble, kind, giving, unselfish, and to accept the fact that we are all equal in posture and presence. It is the total opposite of the "all for me; none for you" power trip we are led to believe we need to be on to "succeed and keep up with our neighbors."

The most profound word of encouragement I can offer for leaders to inculcate the Golden Rule is that it is the total antithesis of the philosophy of those leaders who are autocratic, abrupt, and rude.

By practicing the Golden Rule, you will intrinsically and naturally be compassionate and reasonable in your judgment and propositions. Without a word, the very deportment of your relationships will acknowledge that everyone needs to be related to in a civilized, respectful way, which is dignifying and encouraging.

People in an organization will ascribe to, and model, the tone and tenor that is displayed by their leaders. Leaders must stay cognizant that their discipline to talk to and treat others as they desire to be spoken to and treated has a huge impact that ripples into all manner of impact. This is networking and "paying forward" at its very best.

As a leader what better yield from the structure of your relationship style could you ask for? By using the Golden Rule, you are literally making the world a better place.

> "Being kind is more important than being right."
> —Andy Rooney

> "If you want others to be happy practice compassion. If you want to be happy practice compassion."
> —The Dalai Lama

> "Treat everyone fairly and they'll help you succeed."
> —Bob Page

65

H

"H"
is for
"Hard Work"

Hard Work

Recently I overheard my son encouraging his daughter to begin a task she had been avoiding. He said to her in these words: "Do the hard work—now!"

- World-renowned architect Frank Lloyd Wright once quipped, "I have known the price of success: dedication, hard work, and an unremitting devotion to seeing things you want to see happen."

- Inventor Thomas Edison exclaimed, "Genius is 1 percent inspiration and 99 percent perspiration!"

- President Calvin Coolidge said, "All growth depends on activity. There is no development physically or intellectually without effort, and effort means work."

Nothing trumps hard work. . . nothing.

One cannot expound about hard work, and the effort it requires without mentioning Malcolm Gladwell's book *Outliers*. In his best-selling book, Gladwell offers that his studies conclude that to be proficient or have expertise at any task requires at least 10,000 hours of effort. In other words, if you work from nine to five every day for five years you can be an "overnight success" like the Beatles or Bill Gates! There are no shortcuts or crash courses; you have to apply yourself and dedicate your effort over a prolonged period of time if you want to be skilled and stand apart. You have to do the hard work.

The compelling phenomenon of hard work is that it levels the playing field. Everyone sets off at the same place and with the same potential; it is its own singular entity. There are always faster, stronger, smarter, richer, better-educated, more proficient, better looking, more in shape, more creative people. But: harder working, more determined, more ready to sacrifice, more committed than you? Nobody can outwork you!

Now!

You must be intrinsically motivated; so you have to find it within yourself to push aside excuses and procrastination, and simply begin. I have found that once you do commence, you quickly realize that the job is not as cumbersome as you thought and that each step of progress and achievement is very satisfying. This spurs you on.

Brian Tracey is very learned in these areas, and he has written, among other works, *Good Goal Quotes*. He shares this point: "The hardest part of any important task is getting started on it in the first place. Once *you* actually begin work on a valuable task you seem to be naturally motivated to continue."

If the situation lends itself to you in some fashion, record your first efforts or the "before" phase. This can be later viewed and can be very revealing and worthwhile feedback. You often find yourself opining in words like these: "Was I really that bad?" But the observable progress is satisfying and motivating.

I encourage you to adopt a sense of pride that you even commit to a task; most people do not even try. Allow your progress to build your confidence and to energize you. Enjoy the process and the experience of satisfaction within yourself.

Strive to do excellent work. I have heard it said, "Excellence costs, but mediocrity costs more."

As Samuel Goldwyn quipped, "The harder I work, the luckier I get!"

I

"I"
is for
"Importance"

Importance

"The main thing is to keep the main thing the main thing."
—Stephen R. Covey

The personal and corporate life of a leader is marked by having to constantly decide, discern, and deliberate on the relative import of facts, data, and information. A leader needs to research and gather a body of data, and then establish the relationship between them and the topic at hand.

From the enumeration of core values and goals, to writing checklists, to finding cause-and-effect dynamics and therefore solutions to problems, to decision-making, to delegating, a leader must be facile in the process of assessment and the discrimination of facts and phenomena.

This facility ensures that attention is focused on what matters, and aids in the efficiency of rendering decisions, and then architectural plans that are succinct and reasoned.

The principles and practices required to act and think about the most pertinent issues and information are achieved through the application and refinement of a matrix or model that is developed over time—and with experience, of course.

Values and Goals

Leaders must develop (and then periodically audit) their individual and organizational vision, values. mission, goals, objectives, and action steps. When the big picture is set and clear, all the other issues can be addressed readily and reliably.

Core Values are the fundamental beliefs, ideals, or practices that inform how a person or organization conducts life. They are the first prism or filter that helps in determining asset allocation, decision making, and plans for growth.

For example, the first core value at APS is safety. Any idea, goal, suggestion, or plan must first and foremost be evaluated for its safety quotient. If a resolve for any safety concerns cannot be thought of or developed, the issue is over—period!

A vision statement is a presentation of a clear focus on the reason for your work. It is the "vivid mental image of what your life or business will be in the future."

The establishment of the program's aspirations that come forth from the vision are collectively the mission and goals of an entity. These become, in essence, a summation of the programs and values. In other words, "Why do you exist?"

Objectives and action steps are developed to effectuate the plans and processes necessary to achieve the goals, and in turn realize the mission and vision that was set forth. Goals should be "SMART": Specific, Measurable, Attainable, Relevant, and Time bound.

Causation and Solutions

A leader strives to address the cause of an issue, rather than its symptoms. By doing so, one can achieve a lasting, reliable remedy and resolve the issue at hand.

Engaging the scientific method is a technique that provides "real" and empirical knowledge and facts. It ensures accurate interpretation through a process employing careful observation, rigorous skepticism, and engaging in the testing of deductions drawn from a hypothesis.

The scientific method includes the following steps: asking a question, doing background research, constructing a hypothesis, testing your hypothesis by doing an experiment, analyzing your data, and drawing a conclusion. Finally, you report results—and that way, you find out whether your hypothesis is correct.

The incorporation of the elements of the scientific method are invaluable in the effort to assess correlations and to determine cause, thus it greatly contributes to achieving accurate conclusions. Subjectivity is intrinsically minimized. This method demands written documentation which, in turn, enhances the process of thorough analysis and a record for future referral.

Decisions

Discernment is the ability to judge well. Judging well and making good decisions are tantamount to successful leadership and life. One probably makes thousands of judgments a day. Even deciding what to ponder, and ultimately make a decision on, is a crucial judgment in itself!

> Will Rogers once quipped, "Wisdom and success are garnered by making good decisions. Making good decisions is learned by having made bad decisions."

> William James observed, "The art of being wise is the art of knowing what to overlook."

Establishing a decision-making model or matrix is of extreme import for an entrepreneurial leader. It takes thought, time, and experience. Your model for making decisions provides for a process to take information and facts, filter them, rank them—all in order to see that, through critical thinking, you can be confident in your final judgment.

Here are some building blocks that should aid your process for developing a strategy or formula for your thoughtful analysis in assessing the problems and challenges you are addressing.

Identify your personal core values and be cognizant of your organization's core values. Avoid, at all costs, deviating from these values. Consider them moral absolutes to the point whereby any solution that violates even one of them must be eliminated from a potential consideration. If you lean toward rationalization or "situation ethics" (i.e., values are subjective and flexible, depending on the particulars of a situation) you invite subjectivity to play a role and this leads to inconsistency and eventually detracts from having others trust your opinions. People do not respect either a double standard or the employ of prejudice in a leader's thinking and/or conclusions. I have found that being fair and forthright ultimately demonstrates to your followers that you possess integrity and clarity in your thoughts. Even if they might disagree, they will respect your opinion and respectfully comply.

Be very guarded to not rush to judgment on any topic under

consideration, especially if some outside influence is suggesting that you must. There is always another deal and another option!

In this same vein, do not make a decision until you absolutely must or you are confident. Take advantage of any length of time you are afforded to exercise your due diligence in gathering data and other pertinent information and answers to inquiries. Then digest and filter this body of knowledge. The more informed you are, the greater the probability of a wise judgment resulting. Time is your ally. Take all the time you need.

Leaders often experience pressure and intimidation from others. When people, even your followers, coerce you or threaten your confidence and peace, remain calm. Do not give them the satisfaction their ill-spirited tactics are seeking. I have often tried to defuse or even retaliate against these actions and behaviors by quietly expressing how surprised (and even shocked) I am to hear them express such sentiments, for I always have held the opinion that they are reasonable, fair, and successful people. I find that this tactic succeeds and often leads to contrition and a civil demeanor going forward, for they desire to live up to this positive perception of them I have described.

Finding a quiet space alone, or going for a walk, can be a fruitful endeavor to clear your head, breathe, relax, and think deliberately. Turn off the appliances and think!

Recoil from any thought that your decision has to be, or can be, perfect. As with all endeavors, you will never be perfect at decision making. Some will be wrong. Convince yourself that perfection is the enemy of good and progress. You are a courageous leader and you have done your homework, making your best judgment with the most audited data available to you. If you are correct 1 percent more than you are wrong you will be a winner!

Reflect on the 80/20 theory. If your decision addresses 80 percent of the issue, engage it. There is risk in every judgment. You can mollify this risk by subjecting the solution to is this with "for the greater good" filter. If you are loyal to your values and the greater good can be served, with no one injured, then a decision to keep progress moving forward can and should be made with confidence and courage.

A few final thoughts regarding data

When analyzing data, seek out its source and dissect its reliability and validity.

Focus your initial thinking on the mean—the average. Do not be distracted by the proverbial "two ends of the bell curve" of the data. In these cases, you must also muse on whether the data or topic being researched is just correlated or if indeed it is causal; and to what extent. Always attempt to address cause and not symptom.

In a similar vein, strive to establish within the body of information you have obtained a hierarchy or priority list employing a numerical ranking system as to the weight or importance of each piece under consideration. Numbers are reliable and objective.

During an interview a reporter asked the bank president for the secret to success. Here is how the conversation went:

"Two words."
"And what are they?"
"Right decisions."
"How are right decisions made?"
"One word."
"What is that?"
"Experience."
"How do you get experience?"
"Two words."
"What are they?"
"Wrong decisions."

J

"J"
is for
"Joint Efforts"

Joint Efforts

Joint efforts encompass any endeavor where there is more than one person taking on the task at hand. For example, it could be a task force, committee, or other assigned body within an organization or it could also be when two entities form a partnership, alliance, joint venture, consortium, or any other formal collaborative group. Today, the current vernacular often used to define and describe an assembly of bodies for a combined effort is TEAM.

Together
Everyone
Accomplishes
More

Ben Zander, the famous British maestro and motivational speaker, states: "Leaders need to work to orchestrate others to passion, creativity, and desire to contribute."

The collective effort of a spirited, well-led team is a very satisfying experience. The feeling of being a valued, contributing member of a team is very motivating and rewarding. Discerning the need to form a group or bring others together requires a confident, "I cannot do it all" entrepreneurial leader, as you have to subordinate and, as Elia Gaynor Minden said, "Be humble and open-minded, actively seek advice and support." You must acknowledge that no one can do it alone. A strong ego needs to be chastened and a grateful heart and mind must come forth in words and accolades to the group. Self-centeredness needs to be stifled.

One of the most beneficial groups for a leader to bring together is that where the charge is to "brainstorm." Brainstorming is most usually defined as a forum which gathers a group together to focus on exercising creativity of thoughts and ideas to seek solutions or conclusions.

Creativity is the fuel that propels new products, systems, ideas, and solutions. Effective leaders are often creative themselves, but gathering a body together to jointly think and share on the topic is a very profitable and proven method to seek fresh notions and to problem solve.

For me the concept of brainstorming was greatly aided when I learned that the Spanish definition is a "rain of ideas." In brainstorming sessions, groups prepare a list of ideas shared spontaneously by the members with each member contributing his or her thoughts and creative energies.

A group of four to seven persons is most effective for brainstorming. The use of brainstorming by a leader is prudent, for it may not only provide resolve for the mission at hand but the very process is a tool to aid in developing a culture of inclusivity and respect—one which encourages creativity and enhances the confidence of the group and in each of the members as they go about their individual efforts for the company. It is a great team building exercise. Just being invited to join the assembly has many redeeming effects on people.

Miha Matlievski has written four simple rules for brainstorming sessions which I believe capture the essence of the trust and collaboration that needs to be present and employed for the team to succeed.

- No judgments. Discard no idea.

- Think freely—ideas are neither silly nor impossible.

- Big Numbers—the more ideas the better—strive for at least 20 of them.

- Many heads are better than one—Be accepting of all ideas and the people offering them.[5]

The most thorough and practical writing on brainstorming I have encountered is a piece by Briana Hansen dated May 16, 2018 and found on the website www.wrike.com. It is a necessary read for

---

5 https://www.fail.coach/2016/08/09/brainstorming/

a leader in order to understand and improve the employment and facilitation of brainstorming.

I quote the following from the article.

"You can design and create, and build the most wonderful place in the world. But it takes people to make the dream a reality."
—Walt Disney

Does brainstorming ever feel like a total waste of time? You believe it's necessary to get your team's input on a topic, but the session usually just turns into a few people bickering, and the other participants saying nothing at all.

Even if it was a good session with solid ideas, the meeting notes (if there are any) will most likely end up lost in an email chain abyss never to be found again.

These are classic examples of brainstorming gone wrong.

When venturing into the world of brainstorming, keep a few important things in mind.

First, the top priority of brainstorming is quantity over quality. Yes, you read that right: quantity, not quality. Brainstorming is the first step in the exploration phase of a new project, so it's important to be open to all ideas and possibilities. Problems arise when team members filter out the good ideas from the not-so-good ones out of a fear of rejection or judgment.

Another problem with brainstorming is many people think it can only be done one way: an open discussion in a meeting room with everyone involved. This method is not necessarily wrong, but leads to some largely unrecognized social drawbacks that contribute to an unproductive session.

For instance, when the first couple of ideas are shared during a session, there is a tendency to only focus on those ideas throughout the rest of the meeting.

The biggest problem with brainstorming is only a few people do 60-75 percent of the talking. This bias, often called "anchoring," can often prevent other fresh ideas from coming to light.

Don't get lazy when you brainstorm—keep it both efficient and effective.

Please refer to the article for further information on the seven techniques:

1. Brain Writing
2. Figure Storming
3. Online Brainstorming (Brain-netting)
4. Rapid Ideation
5. Round Robin Brainstorming
6. Starbursting
7. Stepladder Technique[6]

On April 4, 2014, I authored a memo to my staff on brainstorming along with a model I have utilized with success.

Brainstorming

Brainstorming is a group or individual creativity technique by which efforts are made to find a conclusion for a specific problem by gathering a list of ideas spontaneously contributed by its members.

Rules for Brainstorming:

1. FOCUS ON QUANTITY: This rule is a means of enhancing divergent production, aiming to facilitate problem solving through the maxim "quantity breeds quality." The assumption is that the greater the number of ideas generated, the greater the chance of producing a radical and effective solution.

2. WITHHOLD CRITICISM: In brainstorming, criticism of ideas generated should be put on hold. Instead, participants should focus on extending or adding to ideas, reserving criticism for a later critical stage of the process. By suspending judgment, participants will feel free to generate unusual ideas. No one speaks twice until everyone has spoken once.

---

6 https://www.wrike.com/blog/techniques-effective-brainstorming/

3. WELCOME UNUSUAL IDEAS: To get a good and long list of ideas, unusual ideas are welcomed. They can be generated by looking from new perspectives and suspending assumptions. These new ways of thinking may provide better solutions.

4. COMBINE AND IMPROVE IDEAS: Good ideas may be combined to form a single better good idea, as suggested by the slogan "1+1=3." It is believed to stimulate the building of ideas by a process of association.

I desire that we become a company that practices brainstorming. If you see a repeated specific problem and want some ideas, ask your supervisor to arrange for a brainstorming session. Let's all be willing to sit in on a session if called upon.

I suggest we start by learning the nominal group technique. In it, participants are asked to write their ideas anonymously. Then the facilitator collects the ideas and the group votes on each idea. The vote can be as simple as a show of hands in favor of a given idea. This process is called distillation.

After distillation, the top-ranked ideas may be sent back to the group or to subgroups for further brainstorming. For example, one group may work on the color required in a product. Another group may work on the size, and so forth. Each group will come back to the whole group for ranking the listed ideas. Sometimes, ideas that were previously dropped may be brought forward again once the group has reevaluated the ideas.

No Idea is unworthy of consideration; Share

A final comment on the topic of creativity and the corporate and individual growth attained through adoption of brainstorming and unified commitment to a "possibility" (anything is possible) mindset and culture would be to reflect on the national bestseller written by Benjamin Zander and Rosamund Stone Zander, *The Art of Possibility: Transforming Professional and Personal Life*. In the book, the Zanders present the twelve breakthrough practices for bringing creativity and a sense of possibility into all endeavors.

An informative article authored by James Clear regarding this book can be found on this website—

https://jamesclear.com/book-summaries/the-art-of-possibility

Mr. Clear does a masterful job of summarizing and in doing so wetting the appetite to partake of this book. To give you a clear sense, here is a quote:

The Book in Three Sentences

Everything in life is an invention. If you choose to look at your life in a new way, then suddenly your problems fade away. One of the best ways to do this is to focus on the possibilities surrounding you in any situation rather than slipping into the default mode of measuring and comparing your life to others.

The Art of Possibility Summary

- If it's all invented, then you might as well invent a way of viewing life that benefits you. You might as well invent a frame of possibility.

- Give an A. If you automatically assume the best and give everyone and A in life, then you let the best come out in them and you remove a lot of the barriers that have been keeping the relationship back.

- Nearly everyone lives in The Measurement World without realizing it. Everything we do is based on measurement in our lives. How much money we make. Whether our team wins. How beautiful our spouse is. Everything is based around some form of measurement.

- You don't need to play the measurement game. You can play the possibility game. You can live in The Possibility World.

- Instead of focusing on how you measure up, focus on how you contribute to the world around you. Contribution is not measured based on other people. It's only measured based on what you put into the world around you. That's it. If you add something, you contributed.

- Assignment for yourself: write down all the ways in which you have been a contribution to the world around you in the last week. There is no space for your failures or missteps. You only get to list how you contributed in a positive way.

- A leader who feels he is superior is likely to suppress the visions of the very people he needs to rely on to succeed.

- The conductor can lead the most powerful orchestra in the world, but does not make a sound. His or her only power is in getting the players to produce the beautiful sound they are capable of.

- What would I say if I were suddenly called upon to lead?

- How much greatness to expect of those around us? It matters.

- Don't take yourself so damn seriously.

- If you are worried about making a mistake, then imagine that a 500-pound cow will fall on your head.

- The Calculating Self is who runs our lives in The Measurement World. The Central Self is who runs our lives in The Possibility World.

- What would have to change to make this possible?

- Redraw the box in your mind to create a reference frame that embraces the way things actually are and allows you to see them in a new way.

- Zander's music professor said to him when he struggled to learn a new piece quickly: "You mean, you've been playing for THREE MINUTES and you STILL haven't mastered it?"

- Be with the way things are. We have to distinguish our thoughts and feelings about the events from how the events actually are. We often let our feelings separate our conclusions about events from our descriptions of the events themselves.

- The more attention you shine on the subject, the more evidence of it you find. This is how downward spiral talk escalates into a reality.

- People who describe the glass as half full are not delusional optimists. In fact, they are more based in reality because they are describing a substance that is actually in the glass. They are describing reality as it is. The cynic who describes the glass as half empty is focusing his or her energy on something that is not actually there.

- It is the framework of scarcity—the belief that it exists—that causes divisions between people, not actual scarcity.

- Don't focus on being the best in the world. Focus on being the best FOR the world.

Partnerships

The joining together of two or more individuals or corporate organizations is often advisable for their mutual benefit and gain. Although most entrepreneurial leaders want and need to make it on their own, there are situations where unity of effort and commitment aids every participant's efforts and success. These amalgams require much thought, time, effort, and capital.

Doing your homework and due diligence is key. Deal with as many facts as you can avail yourself with and do not lean on conjecture or stories. Keep a written journal of everything, especially the pros and cons as they are revealed. Any plan that evolves should be subject to a reader as "what if this goes wrong" assessment. The risks must be investigated and contingency plans formulated for as many of them as possible. It always comes down to money. Be certain that distribution of funds programs are as equal as possible. If one party gets the expenses the others should get the cash equivalent.

The professional involvement and counsel of lawyers and accountants is a must.

Lessons From the Geese[7]

This Fall, when you see geese heading south for the winter flying along in "V" formation, you might consider what science has discovered as to why they fly that way.

> FACT: As each bird flaps its wings, it creates an "uplift" for the bird immediately following. By flying in a "V" formation, the whole flock has at least 71 percent greater flying range than if each bird flew on its own.

---

7   Written by Angeles Arrien (1940-2014)

Lesson: People who share a common direction and sense of community can get where they are going more quickly and easily because they are traveling on the thrust of one another.

FACT: When a goose flies out of formation, it suddenly feels that drag and resistance of trying to go it alone. It quickly gets back into formation to take advantage of the lifting power of the bird in front of it.

Lesson: If we have as much common sense as a goose, we stay in formation with those headed where we want to go. We are willing to accept their help and give our help to others. It is harder to do something alone than together.

FACT: When the lead goose gets tired, it rotates back up into the formation, and another goose flies to the point position.

Lesson: It is sensible to take turns doing the hard and demanding tasks and sharing leadership. As with geese, people are interdependent of each other's skills, capabilities, and unique arrangements of gifts, talents, or resources.

FACT: The geese flying in formation honk from behind to encourage those up front to keep up their speed.

Lesson: We need to make sure our honking is encouraging. In groups where there is encouragement, the production is much greater. The power of encouragement (to stand by one's heart or core values and encourage the heart and core of others) is the quality of honking we seek. We need to make sure our honking is encouraging and not discouraging.

FACT: When a goose gets sick, wounded, or shot down, two other geese will drop out of formation with that goose and follow it down to lend help and protection. They stay with a fallen goose until it dies or is able to fly again. Then, they launch out on their own, or with another formation, to catch up with their flock.

Lesson: If we have the sense of a goose, we will stand by our colleagues and each other in difficult times as well as in good.

K

"K"

is for

"Know Yourself"

Know Yourself

Know Yourself—Be Yourself—Accept Yourself

In 1600 William Shakespeare wrote the play *Hamlet* in which the character Polonius proclaims: "This above all—to thine own self be true." And it follows, as the night the day, "Thou canst not than be false to any man."

Well over four hundred years ago, Shakespeare nailed it! In essence, I read here that you have to know yourself, hold fast to your values, virtues, and convictions; hence, you must be the person you were born to be. In the end, pleasing others is admirable; but being confident, convicted, and comfortable in your own skin leads to success and true peace, happiness, and well-being. You cannot be a "true" person by not being genuine and real—first of all to yourself.

Related to this notion of Shakespeare's is that of Saint Francis De Sales who expounded on self-acceptance that same year. He said, "Have patience with all things but first with yourself. Never confuse your mistakes with your value as a human being. You're a perfectly valuable, creative, worthwhile human being simply because you exist. And no amount of triumphs or tribulations can change that. Unconditional self-acceptance is the core of a peaceful mind."

Centuries later, Christian writer Henri Nouwen expressed in several writings: "You are not what you have, what you do, or what other people think about you; you are a beloved child of God and that is all you'll ever need to know to rest and feel worthy." He implored everyone to be the best they can be.

Avoid at all costs falling prey to the judgment of others; unfortunately, it is rarely offered in love and with care or compassion. Be yourself; be proud.

Positive   Positive
Resilient   Resilient
Open   Interested
Unselfish   Diligent
Diligent   Engaged

It is particularly challenging in this world we live in, so replete with social media, mad men, pop culture, and political correctness; to be confident, thoughtful leaders who are transparent and honest in their words and dealings, speaking boldly and with conviction. This is, ironically, just what followers desire from their leaders. Truth builds trust. A leader must be comfortable in living up to the prolific adage spoken by Alexander Hamilton: "If you stand for nothing you will surely fall for anything."

Knowing yourself—your personality, characteristics, values, strengths, and weaknesses—helps define and shape your leadership style and manner. It contributes greatly to your aim to lead with integrity and to model confidence. These goals evolve from you being cognizant of who you are and what assets you can deliver to your relationships and ventures. Knowing when you need to supplement areas which challenge you or do not complement your style and competencies is difficult; but vital to progress and growth in you—and in turn, to your followers. A leader has to gain maturity and become vulnerable and accessible in spirit. A leader must be able to deal honestly with himself or herself as readily as with others. This spirit aids people in determining where they can contribute and it motivates them by allowing them to observe how, and where, they can be of worth to their leader's efforts.

Personality Traits and Assessment Tools

Hippocrates is credited with first discussing personality when he suggested in 460 BC that humans have a persona—a personality that was comprised of four distinct temperaments.

Through the centuries, continued thinking and study has been given to this quest of identifying a person's personality traits for testing, assessment, and evolving new theories.

There are dozens of assessments. There are quizzes such as The Myers-Briggs test. There are assessments which ascertain proclivity to various personality types such as the sixteen personalities and the big five based tests, as well as IQ tests.

By availing yourself of the many writings on this subject, and by actually engaging in some assessments, you learn not only about your nature and personality but also gain insights into types of traits and personality types of others. From this knowledge and experience will spring forth your ability to be more understanding and compassionate and be the leader you aspire to be. Your awareness of people and their traits, strengths, and weaknesses will be invaluable to you as you grow in your management skills as pertains to finding the best jobs and positions for people that complement them and ensure their satisfaction, achievement, and growth for them as well as for your organization.

Most of my experience in this field has been with the Riso-Hudson Enneagram Type Indicator (RHETI). The current version, "2.5" RHETI is regarded as the world's most popular Enneagram-based test. It is scientifically validated, forced choice personality test with 144 paired statements. The test takes forty minutes to complete. It produces a full personality profile across all nine identified types of personality. It provides a unique portrait, indicating the relative strengths and weaknesses of the nine types within your overall personality.

Below are the nine types of personalities assessed in RHETI:

1. THE REFORMER—the rational, idealistic type. Principled. Purposeful. Self-controlled and Perfectionist;

2. THE HELPER—the caring, interpersonal type: Demonstrative, Generous, People Pleasing, and Possessive;

3. THE ACHIEVER—the success-oriented, pragmatic type: Adaptive, Excelling, Driven, and Image Conscious;

4. THE INDIVIDUALIST—the sensitive withdrawn type: Expressive, Dramatic, Self-absorbed and Temperamental;

5. THE INVESTIGATOR—the intense, cerebral type: Perceptive, Innovative, Secretive, and Isolated;

6. THE LOYALIST—the committed, security-oriented type: Engaging, Responsible, Anxious, and Suspicious;

7. THE ENTHUSIAST—the busy, fun-loving type: Spontaneous, Versatile, Distractible, and Scattered;

8. THE CHALLENGER—the powerful, dominating type: Self-Confident, Decisive, Willful, and Confrontational;

9. THE PEACEMAKER—the easygoing, self-effacing type: Receptive, Reassuring, Agreeable, and Complacent.

On January 19 2020, Heather Harper updated her very comprehensive ranking order of the twenty best personality tests. It can be found on the www.workstyle.io/best-personality-test site. It would be certain that any one of these tests, because of their varied emphases and theories, will aid you in your specific assessment goals and desired understandings.

Another revealing assessment is to consider if you are right-brain or left-brain oriented. There are tests that evaluate your productivity to be one or the other. Although the science is not exact, if you study the traits, you will probably be able to see which hemisphere is most defining as to your thoughts, cognitive skills, and personality.

LEFT-BRAIN FUNCTIONS	RIGHT-BRAIN FUNCTIONS
Uses logic	Uses feelings
Detail oriented	"Big picture" oriented
Facts rule	Imagination rules—creative
Words and language	Symbols and images
Math and science	Philosophy & religion
Can comprehend	Can "get it" (i.e., meaning)
Knowing	Believes
Acknowledges	Appreciates
Order/pattern perception	Spatial perception
Knows object name	Knows object function
Reality based	Fantasy based

Forms strategies	Presents possibilities
Practical	Impetuous
Safe	Risk taking

I want to offer a brief introduction to what are called *Positive Affirmations: Self Talk Through Life's Ups and Downs*. This therapeutic paradigm is related to the school of cognitive therapy—the "change the tape in your head" psychology. In short, you become what you think about and dwell on. If it is negative and self-destructive, change it to a positive and affirming inner dialogue.

Our local hospital in Doylestown, PA, recently offered a report on the power of positive affirmations. It instructs that positive affirmation is a short motivational phrase or statement that, when repeated, often becomes in essence a self-fulfilling and prophetic reality. Your future orientation can be influenced by incorporating positive affirmations into your routine and self-talk.

Positive Affirmation:
Self Talk Through Life's Ups and Downs[8]

- I Am Enough;

- I Believe in ME;

- I Am Worthy of Love;

- I Am on My Side;

- I Take Care of Myself;

- My Heart Knows;

- I Forgive ______________ (your name).

8 https://www.doylestownhealth.org/about/news/health-news-and-blog/positive-affirmations-self-talk-through-lifes-ups-and-downs

List some affirmations that you feel would benefit you:

____

____

____

____

____

____

Leaders put themselves into the arena of likely being questioned and criticized. These occasions can deepen normal feelings of self-doubt and loss of confidence. Build your self-image with positive comments to yourself in a deliberate way.

With compassion, when you become aware of the struggles of others, encourage them by offering an affirmation they may employ. We all struggle and can benefit from a kind word or gesture.

Why is it essential to ruminate on positive thoughts? Because you become your thoughts.

Be mindful of your thoughts
For your thoughts become your words

Be mindful of your words
For your words become your actions

Be mindful of your actions
For your actions become your habits

Be mindful of your habits
For your habits become your character

Be mindful of your character
For your character becomes your destiny
—Lao Tzu

Marcel Proust was born in 1871 and died in 1922. He was a French novelist, essayist, and critic. In today's parlance, we would describe him as an influencer.

I have copied his famous questionnaire here. It originated as a parlor game but Proust believed that, in answering these questions, an individual reveals his or her true nature. Give it a go! It is fun and revealing its own way.

- What is your idea of perfect happiness?
- What is your greatest fear?
- What is the trait you most deplore in yourself?
- What is the trait you most deplore in others?
- Which living person do you most admire?
- What is your greatest extravagance?
- What is your current state of mind?
- What do you consider the most overrated virtue?
- On what occasion do you lie?
- What do you most dislike about your appearance?
- Which living person do you most despise?
- What is the quality you most like in a man?
- What is the quality you most like in a woman?
- Which words or phrases do you most overuse?
- What or who is the greatest love of your life?
- When and where were you happiest?
- Which talent would you most like to have?
- If you could change one thing about yourself, what would it be?
- What do you consider your greatest achievement?
- If you were to die and come back as a person or a thing, what would that be?
- Where would you most like to live?
- What is your most treasured possession?
- What do you regard as the lowest depth of misery?
- What is your favorite occupation?

- What is your most marked characteristic?
- What do you most value in your friends?
- Who are your favorite writers?
- Who is your hero of fiction?
- Which historical figure do you most identify with?
- Who are your heroes in real life?
- What are your favorite names?
- What is it that you most dislike?
- What is your greatest regret?
- How would you like to die?
- What is your motto?

World View

An efficient and thoughtful way to get to know people is to query them to ascertain their "world view." A world view is that particular philosophy of, and principles adhered to, by one regarding life in the big-picture perspective. It is a person's understanding and conception of the world and all its dynamics. Each of us attempts to sort out this meaning. What is life and what makes the world tick? We also contemplate our role and place in this world. A world view is the foundation of the nature of your relationship with others, nature, religion, science, history, and being yourself.

My world view: I believe we exist in a universe that was designed and formed by an all-knowing, all-capable, always-present, loving God. I believe that God offers and exercises an unconditional parental love for everyone. This means then that most of our knowledge and character is developed through lessons garnered via hard work and sacrifices, all according to God's plan. God, through His Son, Jesus, teaches us how to truly live, relate, serve, and love others. I strive to be His follower, which means a life dedicated to learning about, and emulating Him; committed to service and justice for all. He is not interested in my ability but my availability. He simply wants me (and you) to have a re-lationship with Him. He asks us to act compassionately—partic-ularly by caring for, and loving the earth, and everyone living on it, especially those who lack opportunity and/or who are treated unjustly.

Take some time and write down your world view.

L

"L"
is for
"Leadership"

Leadership

At the heart of the alphabet, is the heart of our study, L, for leadership. I have been researching, studying, reflecting upon, and practicing leadership for sixty years. In the following pages, I offer several definitions, common characteristics, and theories on leadership. They speak to the depth and breadth of this topic.

Taken together, my hope is that this eclectic survey will coagulate into some ideas and models for you to identify with, and from which you can formulate your own unique style and its subsequent practices.

Wikipedia describes leadership as the "process in which one person can enlist the aid and support of others in the accomplishment of the common task."[9] Wikipedia also quotes Alan Keith of Genentech, who states: "Leadership is ultimately about creating a way for people to contribute to making something extraordinary happen."[10]

A final definition is that of Ken "SKC" Ogbonnia, who says, "Effective leadership is the ability to successfully integrate and maximize available resources within the internal and external environment for the attainment of organizational or societal goals."[11]

To commence our survey of theories, styles, and traits I suggest perusing this taken directly from Wikipedia:

9 https://www2.cdc.gov/cdcup/library/newsletter/CDC_UP_Newsletter_v5_i4.htm

10 See https://www.sbm.com.sa/content/leadership

11 https://www.ukessays.com/essays/business/leadership-styles-and-characteristics-and-management-skills-business-essay.php#

Theories

- ATTRIBUTE PATTERN APPROACH—Based on theorists' arguments that the influence of individual characteristics on outcomes is best understood by considering the person as an integrated totality rather than a summation of individual variables.

- BEHAVIORAL AND STYLE THEORIES—The leader is aloof from participation in work but offers personal praise and criticism for work done.

- SITUATIONAL AND CONTINGENCY THEORIES—The times make the leader; leadership behavior becomes a function of the characteristics of a leader and follower.

- FUNCTIONAL THEORY—The leader's main job is to see that whatever is necessary to group needs is taken care of. The leader brings cohesion to the group.

- TRANSACTIONAL AND TRANSFORMATIONAL THEORIES—The manager/leader is given power to reward or punish based on the team's performance.

- EMOTION—Leadership is an emotionally-laden process; the mood or effect of the leader is impactful.

- NEO-EMERGENT THEORY—Espouses that leadership is created by the emergence of information by the leader or other stakeholders, not through the true actions of the leader himself.

Styles

- AUTOCRATIC OR AUTHORITARIAN—All decision-making powers are centralized in the leader-dictator.

- PARTICIPATIVE OR DEMOCRATIC—Decision-making by a group.

- LAISSEZ-FAIRE OR FREE-REIN—Leader does not lead, but leaves group to itself, thus, giving maximum freedom to subordinates.

- NARCISSISTIC LEADERSHIP—Leadership style in which the leader is only interested in himself/herself; their priority is self—at the expense of their people/group members.

- Toxic Leadership—Leader abuses the leader/follower relationship prior to leading the group and a worse off condition occurs than when he/she first found them.

A much more practical view of leadership is offered by Charles T. Jones who in 1968 wrote his classic *Life is Tremendous*. In this work, Jones preaches that enthusiasm makes all the difference in leadership. He very eloquently captures the dynamics of leadership when he says:

> Leadership. . . is probably the most misunderstood word in our vocabulary today. Leadership is not personality. Leadership is not a position, nor is leadership endowed to a certain few. Leadership is that certain something that is "bought with a price." Bought with a price that can be paid by anyone, and YOU are as much a leader today as you're going to be, because the price you are paying today is determining the leader you will be tomorrow. Everyone has an obligation as well as a privilege in leading something. Leadership begins with a simple decision to pay the price and ends the moment you cease to pay it. The price—loneliness, weariness, abandonment, and vision.

You can be happy, involved, relevant, productive, healthy, and secure for the development of certain personal qualities which make up the traits of leadership. Leaders are made—not born.

First, leadership is learning to live. Leadership is nothing more than really living.

Second, learning to live begins with developing positive attitudes and your inner vision first. You must be learning to say something positive in everything that happens.

Third, by learning to "See it Big and Keep it Simple."

Jones further articulates what he defines as the *Seven Laws of Leadership*.

1. Learning to get excited about your work—"No job can make you, but anyone who can add excitement into theirs can make a job."

2. Use or lose—God gave you attributes and talent—use them and they will grow. "No one is a failure until they blame someone else."

3. Production to Perfection—Don't do anything because it has to be perfect. "Production will teach you a little bit about perfection, but perfection will never be more than your own fantasy."

4. Give to get—leadership is learning to give whether you get anything or not.

5. Exposure to experience—"The experienced person gets to know which keys unlock which doors, while the inexperienced person doesn't know if he even has a key."

6. Flexible planning—"Plan on going wrong."

7. Motivated to motivating—"Our problem is not motivating them, but keeping them from demotivating us. The motivation will flow when you are totally committed and involved."

Additional Musings

Only three things happen naturally within organizations:

1. Friction;

2. Confusion;

3. Underperformance.

"Everything else requires leadership."
—Peter Drucker

"You are a leader if your actions inspire others to dream more, to do more, and become more."
—John Quincy Adams

"A genuine leader is not a searcher for consensus but a molder of consensus."
—Martin Luther King, Jr.

"A vision, or view of the future, is an ongoing, evolving, hopeful look into the future that stirs the hearts and minds of people who knew they will never see the end."
—Ken Blanchard and Bill Hybels, from *Lead Like Jesus.*

"A leader creates the future picture of success."
—A New Equilibrium, Inc.

My Thoughts

A leader knows where he's going and can cause others to go with him.

A leader is often deliberate about keeping himself in a controlled state of urgency.

A leader has "inspiring influence."

A leader has vision; he often creates his own crisis!

Some Other Quotes

"Scholars who have studied the development of leaders have situated resilience, the ability to sustain ambition in the face of frustration, at the heart of potential leadership growth. More important than what happened to them was how they responded to these reversals, how they managed in various ways to put themselves back together, how these watershed experiences at first impeded, then deepened, and finally and decisively molded their leadership."
—Doris Kearns Godwin from her book *Leadership* published in 2020

"Daniel Goleman found that while the qualities traditionally associated with leadership such as intelligence, toughness, determination, and vision are required for success, they are insufficient. Truly effective leaders are also distinguished by a high degree of emotional intelligence, which includes self-awareness, self-regulation, motivation, empathy and social skill."
—Harvard Business Review, January 2004. *What Makes a Leader* by Daniel Goleman

I would suggest that the most significant inclusion of emotional intelligence as a suggested quality to be embraced by leaders would be found in a faith-based assessment of leadership. Michael Youssef is a pastor in Atlanta, Georgia, and he has written *The Leadership Style of Jesus*. It is a very principled study; but it is very applicable and practical. The following is a copy of the Table of Contents. Surveying it will allow you to gain an understanding of what Youssef explores and expands upon. This perusal will allow you to decide as to you reading this fine work.

PART 1: THE BEGINNINGS OF LEADERSHIP
1. The Need to Be Confirmed

2. Acknowledging Those Who Have Gone Before

PART 2: THE QUALITIES OF LEADERSHIP
3. The Leader as Shepherd

4. Man's Rules Versus God's Principles

5. Courage

6. Gentleness

7. Generosity

8. Truthfulness

9. Forgiveness

PART 3: THE TEMPTATIONS OF LEADERSHIP
10. Power

11. Ego

Another untraditional trait of leadership that has been studied and articulated recently is "informed intuition." It is a vital construct of decision-making and goal setting. In his book, *The Leaders Checklist,* Michael Useem stresses the "informed" word. In responding to the question of what is "informed intuition," Useem answered:

Useem: There is a lot of research evidence on that. A great argument comes from Malcolm Gladwell, the author of the book called *Blink.* He says intuition is extremely important and vital to have. Gut instinct is a great platform for making good and timely decisions. Having said that, gut instinct, intuition that is not informed by experience, is likely to be a disaster. So when the author of *Blink* writes as a subtitle, *The Power of Thinking Without Thinking,* the subsubtitle should be, *After Having Digested Prior Experience.* And there's just lots of evidence on that.

Question from Knowledge@Wharton: What's an Example?

Useem: Probably the best example that comes to mind very quickly here is what we learned from the United States Marine Corps. As we watch the officers and the officer candidate school train future Marine Corps officers, the teaching method is for people to get out, act, experience, succeed and fail, and then conduct what they call the "After Action Review." To take it apart—what went well? What did not go well? And that is, in my view, one of the great avenues for leadership development—which is to take apart your last day or your last week and reflect on it. After a couple of years of doing those "after action reviews," you can say correctly with confidence, "My intuition tells me right now that I ought to be going in this direction and not that direction."

Question from Knowledge@Wharton: So that's informed intuition?

Useem: Yes, informed intuition. . . informed by your own and others' experiences.

Miller and Blanchard on Serving

A most intriguing and counterintuitive style of leadership is explored in the book *The Secret—What Great Leaders Know and Do* by Mark Miller and Ken Blanchard. In this classic business fable, the authors promote the notion that the secret of great leaders is that "great leaders serve." Note that the new edition of this book includes a leadership self-assessment so that readers can measure to what extent they lead by serving.

Utilizing a brisk question-and-answer format, the authors develop their posture around an initialism: S.E.R.V.E.

S   **S**ee the Future

Leaders must help the people they lead see the destination, as well as the advantages of going there. Everybody needs to see who they are, where they are going and what will guide their journey.

E   **E**ngage and Develop others

Do whatever it takes to engage in the hearts and the heads of the people. Get the right players on the team.

R   **R**einvent Continuously

This is where our value in creativity can really shine. The

leader must be willing to reinvent on at least three levels. The first is personal. Some key questions to ask are "How am I learning and growing as a leader? What am I doing to encourage others in my group to constantly learn and reinvent themselves?"

The second level of reinvention is systems and processes. We must ask ourselves and our people, "How are we doing the work? How can we do it better? What changes would enhance our ability to serve our customers and each other?"

The third type of reinvention involves the structure of the organization. A good question to ask here is "What structural changes do we need to make to be more efficient and effective?" Leaders must always ask these types of questions.

V   **Value Results and Relationships**

We value our customers first, and that value guides our behavior and ensures our continuing success.

E   **Embody the Values**

If we lose our credibility as leaders, our leadership potential will be greatly limited. You must do more than articulate the values, although I believe that it is very important. We must not only say it—we must show it.

In their book, Miller and Blanchard explore deeply principles such as:

- Why great leaders seem preoccupied with the future.
- How people on the team ultimately determine your success or failure.
- What three areas require continuous improvement.
- Why true success and leadership have two essential components.
- How to not legally strengthen or unwittingly destroy leadership credibility.

Any student of leadership will benefit from this important work.

On a personal level I have been afforded the privilege of working with and for some very gifted leaders.

The entrepreneurial minded leaders who have impacted me and my leadership in significant ways are some of those that lead the companies we engage with in business.

Ten years ago, the position of the North American president of our longest standing customer was filled by an army ranger veteran—a graduate of Stern School of Business at N.Y.U. His mentorship, guidance, and our growth together are a gift to me. Below is a copy of a Credo he authored at the request of a newly appointed CEO.

He models a form of leadership that is dedicated to stating his credo in goals, auditing them often and amending them as needed. He is completely transparent and confident because of his adherence to strong, stated principles.

I share it with thanks, and urge you to study it for its concise and thoughtful content. Priorities are declared and bold leadership is committed.

We should all take a moment and articulate our credo.

Your attending to every word will provide for you a treasure trove of information, management techniques, and the wisdom of a very successful business leader.

Business Credo:

1. Start with the consumer.

2. Average organizations give people something to work on— Great organizations give people something inspiring to work toward.

3. If you don't know where you are going, any road may get you there.

4. We can try to do anything, just not everything. We need to be ruthless on priorities, or we will be forced to be ruthless on people.

5. We have no money to spend, only to invest. Always have a plan for a return on investment. If half of our plans work, we are heroes.

6. Debate candidly. Decide cohesively. One team.

7. It's simple (or should be), just not easy.

Absorb the principles of leadership that are practiced by those who deal with life-and-death issues. In their book *Extreme Ownership*, Jocko Willink and Leif Babin articulate how US Navy Seals lead and win.

I quote:

PRIORITIZE AND EXECUTE

On the battlefield, countless problems compound in a snowball effect, every challenge complex and in its own right, each demanding attention. But a leader must remain calm and make the best decisions possible. To do this, SEAL combat leaders utilize Prioritize and Execute. We verbalize this principle with this direction: "Relax, look around, make a call."

BUILD TRUST WITH YOUR MEMBERS

Trust is not blindly given. It must be built over time. Situations will sometimes require that the boss walk away from a problem and let junior leaders solve it, even if the boss knows he might solve it more efficiently. It is more important that the junior leaders are allowed to make decisions—and backed up even if they don't make them correctly. Open conversations build trust. Overcoming stress and challenging environments builds trust. Working through emergencies and seeing how people react builds trust.

LEADING DOWN THE COMMAND

As a leader employing Extreme Ownership, if your team isn't doing what you need them to do, you first have to look at yourself. Rather than blame them for not seeing the strategic picture, you must first figure out a way to better communicate it to them in terms that are simple, clear, and concise, so that they understand. This is what leading down the chain of command is all about.

Leading UP the command. Don't ask your leader what you should do, tell them what you are going to do.

If your boss isn't making the decision in a timely manner or providing necessary support for you and your team, don't blame the boss. First, blame yourself. Examine what you can do better to convey the critical information for decisions to be made and support allocated.

Discipline yourself

Discipline starts every day when the first alarm clock goes off in the morning. I say "first alarm clock" because I have three, as I was taught by one of the most feared and respected instructors in SEAL training: one electric, one battery powered, one wind up. That way, there is no excuse for not getting out of bed, especially with all that rests on that decisive moment. The moment the alarm goes off is the first test; it sets the tone for the rest of the day. The test is not a complex one: when the alarm goes off, do you get up out of bed, or do you lie there in comfort and fall back to sleep? If you have the discipline to get out of bed, you win—you pass the test. If you are mentally week for that moment and you let that weakness keep you in bed, you fail. Though it seems small, that weakness translates to more significant decisions. But if you exercise discipline, that too translates to more substantial elements of your life.

Production:

1. No bad teams, just bad leaders

2. Over-communicate, don't assume

3. Look in the mirror first

Admit and own mistakes and develop plan to overcome them, and blame no one else.

- For leaders, the humility to admit and own mistakes and develop a plan to overcome them is essential to success. The best leaders are not driven by ego or personal agendas. They are simply focused on the mission and how best to accomplish it.

- Own everything in your world, and blame no one else. Embrace Extreme Ownership. Leaders must own everything in their world. There is no one else to blame.

As a Leader, you must demonstrate Extreme Ownership throughout the chain of command.

THERE ARE NO BAD TEAMS, ONLY BAD LEADERS.

- When a bad SEAL leader walked into a debrief and blamed everyone else, that attitude was picked up by subordinates and team members, who then followed suit. They all blamed everyone else, and inevitably the team was ineffective and unable to properly execute the plan. . .

- . . . They see Extreme Ownership in their leaders, and, as a result, they emulate Extreme Ownership throughout the chain of command down to the most junior personnel. As a group they try to figure out how to fix their problems— instead of trying to figure out who or what to blame.

AS LEADER, YOU MUST EXPLAIN NOT JUST WHAT TO DO, BUT WHY. FIND OUT IF YOU DON'T KNOW.

- The leader must explain not just what to do, but why. It is the responsibility of the subordinate leader to reach out and ask if they do not understand. Only when leaders at all levels understand and believe in the mission can they pass that understanding and belief to their teams so that they can persevere through challenges, execute and win. . .

- . . . So, if you ever did the task or guidance or a mission that you don't believe in, don't just sit back and accept it. Ask questions until you understand why so you can believe in what you are doing and you can pass the information down the chain to your team with confidence, so they can get out and execute the mission. That is leadership.

CONTROL YOUR OWN EGO

- Ego clouds and disrupts everything: the planning process, the ability to take good advice, and the ability to accept constructive criticism. It can even stifle someone's sense of self-preservation. Often, the most difficult ego to deal with is your own. . .

- . . . It's natural for anyone in a leadership position to blame subordinate leaders and direct reports when something goes wrong. Our egos don't like to take blame. But it's on us as leaders to see where we failed to communicate effectively and help our troops clearly understand what their roles and responsibilities are and how their actions impact the bigger strategic picture.

SIMPLIFY THE PLAN

- Almost no mission ever goes according to plan. There are simply too many variables to deal with. This is where simplicity is key. If the plan is simple enough, everyone understands it, which means each person can rapidly adjust and modify what he or she is doing. If the plan is too complex, the team cannot make rapid adjustments to it, because there is no baseline understanding of it."

✍

The following pages are emails exchanged between myself and a graduate student in February of 2011. This interview was a significant part of a Leadership Project which was a course requirement. I am hopeful that these questions and answers, generated from the syllabus and definitions being studied, will prove helpful and informative.

February 2011

Mr. Belding,

I hope everything is going well. I was hoping that I could get your opinion on some of these leadership models which we are learning about. If you could just let me know a couple things on each:

1. Where do they believe this approach on leadership is appropriate?

2. If it is, is it universal in principle or does it only work in certain situations?

And then. . .
What model do you most relate to?
Each model is numbered and underneath it is what each of them entails. If you need to know more or anything else just let me know. Thank you again for helping out with this! By the way, there is no rush. Get back to me when you can.
—Audrey

1. COMBAT MODEL OF LEADERSHIP
- Embrace risk (expand opportunity especially with products/market)
- Innovate
- Take charge
- Maintain high expectations
- Be positive
- Get out in front

2. TRAITS MODEL
- Born a leader, cannot learn leadership
- Essential traits: self-confidence, motivation, intelligence

3. METAPHORS OF LEADERSHIP (WHICH ONE MOST RELATES TO YOU AND HOW YOU WORK AT APS?)
- Human resources: emphasis on people, relationships rather than the tasks

- Political: emphasis on resource allocation, negotiation, alliance, and coalition building
- Symbolic: the system vision, culture, values, and inspiration

4. FIVE PRACTICES OF LEADERSHIP

- Model the way
- Inspire a vision
- Challenge the process; take a risk
- Enable others to act
- Encourage the heart

My Response:

A few musings on your leadership project:

As you know I lead a relatively small business that I founded. I am an entrepreneurial leader not a corporate one *per se*. This significantly affects my opinions and perspectives.

1. I think of General Patton as a poster child for this definition! I feel this better describes a corporate leader rather than an entrepreneur in that, often, corporate leaders are mouthpieces. They are the public face of the company projecting its image and delivering the message of the larger corporate goals and strategies. This person personifies and articulates the tone and tenor of the organization. They are often PR oriented.

2. I am not sure anyone is a born leader. Nature and life experiences mold you. When you look at Jobs, Dell, and Gates, etc., you see people who have learned to be leaders and grow organizations. They are obviously first and foremost gifted inventors and thinkers. I tend to think there are certainly some prerequisite character traits and skills that aid in developing leadership skills but practice and experience are the strongest determiners. People must be willing to expose themselves, make themselves vulnerable to risk and they must combat the fear of failure.

In 1 and 2, I see no criteria that address problem-solving abilities nor talks about being able to think critically and adapt. Adaptation and flexibility are essential elements to leadership. Perseverance, diligence and, never-give-up attitudes are key.

1. Each element listed here is employed to some degree by entrepreneurial leaders. One finds oneself in a constant variety of situations which often call for employing different and varied traits and responses. One often "customizes" one's style to complement the audience or the situation. I have employed all three of these domains throughout my tenure.

My personal view of leadership is that ultimately one evolves a style which integrates one's personality, character, and values; in other words, one's genuine self. People follow others for many reasons, good and bad. In the final analysis, successful outcomes from successful people, I find that those result from leadership which is constant and grounded in positive values and goals.

Jim Collins wrote *Good to Great*—a must read. Surprising to him and most others is that the foremost trait of effective leaders is that they possess absolute humility and iron will. This is counterintuitive on many levels! Humility is defined as depending on others, yet iron will takes a strong ego! I say values lead to beliefs, the beliefs to thoughts, thoughts to choices, choices to behaviors, behaviors to performance. It's another way of saying performance (leadership) is grounded in and incepted from values. For me, this is my goal as a Christian. I strive to live by the Golden Rule—to strive to employ in my leadership the creed that I want to treat others the way I would want to be treated. I therefore strive to create a culture (an environment, a society, a spirit) wherein others feel valued, included, and in which they enjoy a sense of continued opportunity and success. Like life itself, never easy, ever complete, but always the goal.

April 2011

Mr. Belding,

I just need a little more of your input to continue with the project. I just have a couple of questions. Again, there is no rush to answer these. I hope all is well and thank you again.

1. In what ways were you influenced to be a leader—did you have a mentor or just an intrinsic motivation to lead?

2. Is the relationship to the subordinates more important or the task at hand? How do you find the balance?

3. What expectations do you have for your subordinates and what do you think they should expect from you?

Thank you again, Mr. Belding!

My Response:

1. I think leadership is a classic case of nature/nurture. My dad constantly reminded us and encouraged us to be bold to do the "right" thing and stand up for those who needed help. I am relatively short in height and I believe that this motivated me. I was confident in my abilities and thoughts, and knew if I did not lead I would be looked over—and not in the game!

2. I would like to think that people and their well-being always supersedes goals or tasks. I have found that ultimately doing the right thing for people yields the best business outcomes as well. That is not to say that sometimes short-term sacrifices are not in order i.e., layoffs for the long-term gain of the company staying in business in the future.

3. May the Golden Rule rule!—"Do unto others as you would have them do unto you."

When I peruse the list of CEOs who have led major corporations with an entrepreneurial inflection and zeal, none stands out more to me than Lee Iacocca.

Mr. Iacocca's influence on business and our country was profound. He was a pioneer in the automotive world—first at Ford where he developed that industry-changing Mustang, and then at Chrysler where he brought that corporation back from a dead-on-arrival state to repaying a government loan early and with interest! At the request of President Reagan, he chaired the committee that restored the Statue of Liberty with private effort and funds.

The story I heard that cements in my mind his entrepreneurial bent and mindset is when Mr. Iacocca wanted to test the market for its willingness to embrace convertibles—vehicles which had fallen out of favor. Harboring an idea that the time was right, Mr. Iacocca called his chief engineer one morning and asked how long it would take to make a convertible prototype of a Chrysler LeBaron. "If we pull out all the stops, sir, four months," came the reply. "Good!" retorted Iacocca. "Grab a hacksaw and make me one by three this afternoon!" As Mr. Iacocca drove his convertible that afternoon, throngs of people waved and cheered. Because of the strong response, orders were given to produce a convertible LeBaron and it became a huge success. Entrepreneurs only have one speed. NOW!

In his book *Where Have All the Leaders Gone?* written along with Catherine Whitney, Mr. Iacocca lays out his "C List" for the prerequisites of being an effective leader.

- CURIOSITY—A leader has to listen to people outside of the "yes sir" crowd in his inner circle. He has to read voraciously. If a leader never steps outside his comfort zone, he grows stale.

- CREATIVE—A leader has to communicate. I'm not talking about running off at the mouth or spouting sound bites. I am talking about facing reality and telling the truth.

- CHARACTER—A leader has to be a person of character. That means knowing the difference between right and wrong and having the guts to do the right thing. Abraham Lincoln once said, "If you want to test a man's character, give him power."

- Courage—A leader must have courage.

- Conviction—To be a leader you've got to have conviction—a fire in your belly. You have got to have passion. You have got to really want to get something done.

- Charisma—A leader should have charisma. I am not talking about being flashy. Charisma is the quality that makes people want to follow you. It's the ability to inspire. People follow a leader because they trust him.

- Competent—A leader has to be competent. You've got to know what you are doing. More important than that, you've got to surround yourself with people who know what they're doing.

- Common Sense—Charlie Beacham said, "The only thing you've got going for you as a human being is your ability to reason and your common sense."

A final perspective I present is from the book entitled *Executive Values* by Kurt Martin Senske, CEO of Lutheran Social Service. Kurt presents his three modes of leadership. He expresses that significance is a leadership mode that is so paramount that it not just a second-half goal; it is deemed to be worthy of full-time attention. He is convinced that it is the suggested mode of leadership we should all pursue.

I quote from the book:

Three Modes of Leadership

In my study of leaders from the executive suite to the parish, and positions in between, I have concluded that every leader operates within one of three modes of leadership: survival, success, or significance. Leaders who are in the survival mode are struggling to keep the doors of their organization open. It is likely that such leaders themselves are living the lives that are out of balance. They are fighting a losing battle with the changing of market forces, clinging to outmoded or ineffective leadership styles, or generally failing to follow the Golden Rule of Leadership. Their talents and passions are not aligned with their current position. These individuals are often inattentive, lack commitment to their work, and produce haphazard results. This category of leader includes those who have essentially retired on the job, counting the days to their retirement or their departure. The fire inside his died and they are living out their days hoping no crisis or opportunities arise while they remain on watch.

The second mode of leadership is characterized by the idea of success. A success mode leader has attained financial success, power, and notoriety, but senses that something is still missing. His or her external display of happiness is shallow and insincere, and it often masks personal angst and fear. This leader may well be terrified at the thought of death or the idea of being alone, and may be on a constant quest for the "fountain of youth" or the latest toy. This leader may use those around him or her as tools to achieve personal goals. Leaders operating in this mood have truly lost any sense of balance—and a connectedness to their faith—and leave behind them lives littered with incidents of alcoholism, depression, troubled children, divorce, and estranged relationships. For them, meaning is connected to their position in life and the size of their bank account. They are living proof of the irony that those who strive for success as an end in itself will never achieve it.

The notion of significance describes the third mode of leadership. Leaders in this mode have discovered their gifts and passion and combine the two through work and family to bring meaning to individual and community life. Such leaders use their positions to add true value to the world and to the lives of others. They truly understand the Golden Rule of Leadership and the importance of balancing faith, life, and work.

⌀

A person who has affected my leadership style to a significant degree is singer/songwriter Bruce Springsteen. I have never met Bruce, but I have very consciously tried to emulate him and his leadership style.

Like Bruce, I grew up in New Jersey. I graduated from Manasquan High School on the Jersey shore. I always loved music. Since I was twelve, I have played drums in several bands. I was the founder, catalyst, and leader of each of the bands. I am self-taught—not that accomplished, but musicians like to play with me because I focus on the backbeat and I do not step on anybody's efforts as they sing or play.

Backstory

In the summer of 1968, I started working at a hotel/cafeteria in the Victorian town of Ocean Grove, New Jersey, which is on the Atlantic Coast at the southern border of Asbury Park. The next summer I was asked to return as the assistant manager of kitchen operations. This proved to be a unique life and leadership-developing experience. I was working twelve hours a day alongside a crew of 40 of the hardest working people imaginable. Many were members of extended families, mostly from Florida, to where they migrated back during the winter months. I was the lone "local guy" in the establishment.

While working at the hotel, during the summer of 1970, Asbury Park suffered and struggled with catastrophic civil unrest. Many homes and businesses were destroyed and, in short order, the boardwalk was closed and a pallor fell over the whole city. Many of our cooks and their families roomed in Asbury, so the impact and terror was deeply felt by all. Helping my staff to navigate these times and to feel safe gave me the opportunity to observe and share with a community, which, in some ways, strengthened as we experienced the trauma together. I continue to try and be a good steward based on what I learned in those days and to apply the lessons to my interactions and citizenship today.

$\wp$

I knew there was a rich music scene in Asbury Park, and I was aware of Bruce and some others at the time, and of their struggles to press on after the unrest. Everyone close to the situation was indelibly moved and circumspect.

I was excited to hear of the release of *Greetings from Asbury Park*, Bruce's first album in early 1973. I was in the middle of graduate school and listening to WMMR, a radio station in Philadelphia. A very influential disc jockey, Ed Sciaky, was playing and promoting *Greetings* and the talent of Bruce, especially noting his live performances.

My first ruminations about Bruce and his debut album were that he was extremely talented and creative but also very brave and bold. The instrumentation, the arrangements, the characters being sung about, the amazing lyricism, his voice, and even the use of the bedraggled city of the Asbury Park in the title was courageous and unorthodox. It was so daring and fresh that I was apprehensive for Bruce. I really wanted him to succeed and be rewarded for all his years of hard work.

My admiration for Bruce has been mostly garnered from attending his shows, reading books and articles, and hearing him interviewed. My fondest memory and story of seeing Bruce was in New Brunswick, New Jersey, at the State Theatre. I have a list of shows from October 1973 and this one is not listed but I'm certain there was one—and I was there!

As the band took the stage, Bruce surveyed the less-than-sold-out audience and told many of us in the balcony to move down and join the others for a more partylike crowd. I then remember him warmly introducing his mom who was present, and then off we went!

For two hours, he directed and took the band and all of us on a journey of great music, stories, and stage presence into "the church of rock and roll revival"!

Bruce had everyone in the palm of his hand as he masterfully shared of himself and what he loves to do. He made us feel connected to him, the band, and each other. The band concluded by playing *Twist and Shout* as Bruce popped a beach ball on the last note—heaven!

I was overwhelmed with Bruce's charisma, passion, energy, commitment to excellence, and his love for his band and his fans.

He is unabashedly devoted to his art and those that love it.

I especially appreciate the chemistry and coordination Bruce has formulated and developed in the band. As with the audience, their eyes and attention are always fixed on Bruce and where he will lead them next. The show is dramatic and arresting as it ebbs and flows. It is always fresh, and you know that every detail has been thoughtfully planned and prepared for. When someone cares about, and loves what he does so much that he makes it look effortless, you appreciate it even more.

It is obvious that Bruce gives everything he has in every endeavor he engages in. You always get his very best. He infuses everyone with hope, positivity, and courage. His commitment to preparation is abundantly obvious.

If you educate yourself as to Bruce's early career, you know of his travails. His first albums were critically acclaimed but did not sell well. He battled legal and management issues that delayed recording and added to the pressure for the next problem. He had been told he needed a hit to become the next Bob Dylan or Van Morrison. The pressure was enormous, but he never succumbed. He inspired everyone by his tenacious work ethic, belief in himself and his talent and judgment, and especially his commitment to his craft.

A true indication of people's love for their craft are the efforts they employee to show their respect and to honor those that went before, and inspired them. Bruce does this with devotion and concrete action.

Gary U.S. Bonds had the top single in 1961 with *Dance till Quarter to Three*. This song, and Gary's sound, was a significant influence on Bruce and bandmate Steve Van Zandt, especially the sax playing of Daddy G. On October 29, 1976 in New York City, Bruce brought Gary up on stage with him and the band.

In April of 1981 (Bruce being thirty-two years old) Bruce and Steve took the initiative to resurrect Gary's career by writing music for him and collaborating on two albums which they produced and played on. Thanks to their time and effort Gary's career was revived.

In another act of generosity, kindness, and homage to their influencers, Bruce and Steve came alongside Darlene Love.

Over a period of years Darlene's story and career have been reborn and energized by Bruce and Steve.

The progression of Darlene being inducted into the Rock and

Roll Hall of Fame in 2011, winning an Oscar in "20 Feet from Stardom", which tells of her and other talented backup singers' story, and recording new music in September 2015—material written by Bruce and Steve is a touching vignette.

In 2019, Barbara and I hosted at our home a dinner/concert fundraiser for our local theater. Darlene Love was the entertainment. I was so fortunate to spend time with her.

Darlene never misses an opportunity to witness to her faith and the need to forgive and forget those who take advantage of us. She is also effusive in her gratitude to God for her life and talent and all the good she has been blessed with—especially Bruce and Steve, who found her working in a Beverly Hills Hotel, befriended her, energized her, and with love and encouragement provided her the opportunity to once again feel valued by them and all of her fans.

By the way, despite a recent hip replacement Darlene sang and danced for two non-stop hours; she blew the roof off!

∅

Longevity and continued success are the visible proofs of competent leadership and direction. The E Street Band is fifty years old and can still "rock the house"!

Bruce writes his music with a genuine tone of compassion both for whom the "story" is about and to those who are listening. He is on an eternal quest to decipher human nature—particularly loneliness and struggle. His music urges us on to be reflective, generous, and good. Bruce is an invaluable influence to generations as he leads his band and his fans with his talent and love through the joy of music.

M

"M"
is for
"Meetings"

Meetings

"A meeting is no substitute for progress."
—Anonymous

It has been my experience that larger corporations are very reliant on meetings. Even in the age of web-based gatherings, much time and energy is spent on them and in them. For most entrepreneurial leaders, meetings need to be held to a minimum and they must be very efficient.

Here are some suggestions to consider as you plan and lead meetings:

- Schedule meetings on an as-needed basis. Regularly scheduled meetings should be constantly audited for their continued importance and relevance.

- Carefully select the persons that need to be present after you have written the agenda that will satisfy the need and purpose of the meeting. Do not worry about people's feelings of being hurt when they are not included. Your ultimate invitation should provide a copy of the agenda and state a firm time allotment so schedules can be maintained. Minutes should be kept and distributed to all that need to know the outcome of the meeting, particularly citing the responsible parties and the timelines established on all agreed points of action. The responsible party for executing the action point should be identified.

- Limit participants to at most six people, including you.

- Arrive early to ensure the room is prepared and any technology you will be using is functioning properly.

- Start the meeting at the appointed hour. This will clearly indicate that the gathering is important and that in the future all the people involved will see to it that they are punctual.

- Commence the meeting with a word of welcome and appreciation and with a brief overview of your vision for the proceedings. Do this in a tone that sets the stage for everyone to emulate.

- Foster camaraderie and encourage everyone to respect each other and to listen with an open mind.

- A helpful admonition is to encourage the group by saying, "We do not all have to agree but we all have to be agreeable."

- Insist that everyone speaks once before anyone speaks twice. Ask of those that do wish to speak to offer a summary of what the previous speaker said and then to add their thoughts. Request that there please be no "war stories" or veering off into tangents not relevant to the subject. A timer can aid in this goal if need be.

- Practice what I call "forness." Simply defined, this is the notion that people state what they are in agreement with or offer a suggestion on what they could be "for," rather than dwell on what they are against. People explaining why they are not for something is not time well spent.

- In so doing, "forness" renders monitoring and measuring consensus an easier task. It significantly reduces the time and effort it takes to seek common ground and resolve.

- Encourage honesty and candor.

- Employ the 80/20 rule. If you obtain agreement on at least 80 percent of a topic, determine if this is adequate enough to become your decision or a time to develop a point of action or next steps. In most cases, this measure of collaboration is fine.

- As in all of your management practices, meetings are an excellent forum to foster the beneficial management credo that you should strive to "praise in public and criticize in private."

- Thank all members for your confidence that each individual will go forth supporting the groups decisions and subordinating their ideas or thoughts that might not have been included in the conclusion made by the group.

With the employ of multiple-person meetings using the Internet, a leader needs to establish protocols for efficiency. Here are some courtesies and suggestions.

- Start and end on time;
- Follow agenda and stay on task;
- Leader starts meeting by saying who is in the room and on call;
- Engage remote callers in conversation;
- Remote callers on mute when not speaking;
- Identify self before speaking;
- Speak loud and clear;
- Eliminate *all* sidebar conversations;
- No eating/no paper shuffling/or any other noise making activity.

N

"N"
is for
"Negotiating"

Negotiating

Volumes have been written about negotiating. It is absolutely certain that every entrepreneur or leader will face multiple opportunities to participate in a host of situations that require settlement, resolution, and agreement. During these times, reason, judgment, and communication skills will be demanded, stretched, and honed. In the end, experience is the best teacher. Do your best and then honestly assess what works and what does not.

I offer the following ideal primer for an initial study of the process of negotiation which is directly taken from the website below.

Negotiating Successfully

Negotiation is a process where two or more parties with different needs and goals discuss an issue to find a mutually acceptable solution. In business, negotiation skills are important in both informal day- to-day interactions and formal transactions such as negotiating conditions of sale, lease, service delivery, and other legal contracts.

Good negotiations contribute significantly to business success, as they:

- Help you build better relationships

- Deliver lasting, quality solutions—rather than poor short-term solutions that are not satisfying the needs of either party

- Help you avoid future problems and conflicts.

Negotiating requires give and take. You should aim to create a courteous and constructive interaction that is a win-win for both parties. Ideally a successful negotiation is where you can make concessions that mean little to you, while giving something to the other party that means a lot to them. Your approach should foster goodwill, regardless of the differences in party interests.

A good negotiation leaves each party satisfied and ready to do business with each other again.

This guide explains why negotiation is important, and outlines strategies and tactics for negotiating well.

Negotiation Skills

Negotiating Successfully

Strong negotiators master written, verbal and non-verbal communication. They adopt a conscious, assertive approach to their communication.

Good negotiators are:

- Flexible
- Creative
- Aware of themselves and others
- Good planners
- Honest
- Win-win oriented
- Good communicators.

Assertive Communication

During a negotiation, you may choose to use a passive, aggressive or assertive communication style. Using an assertive style will help increase your chances of negotiating successful outcomes for your business.

Passive communicators are inclined to use ambiguous language, adopt under-confident body language, and give in to demands too easily.

Aggressive communicators, however, are both confidant and considerate. These communicators are more likely to keep discussion going and facilitate mutually beneficial outcomes. They adopt a strong, steady tone of voice. They are factual, rather than emotional or critical. They describe their views, starting sentences with "I," rather than direct criticisms starting with "You."

Learn about communicating effectively for business: https://www.business.qld.gov.au/running-business/marketing-sales/managing-relationships/communicating-effectively

Tips for Effective Negotiation

Don't:
- Confuse negotiation with confrontation—you should remain calm, professional and patient

- Become emotional—remember to stick to the issue, don't make it personal, and avoid becoming angry, hostile or frustrated

- Blame the other party if you can't achieve your desired outcome

Do:
- Be clear about what you are offering and what you need from the other party

- Be prepared—think about what the other party needs from the deal, and take a comprehensive review of the situation

- Be consistent with how you present your goals, expectations and objectives

- Set guidelines for the discussion and ensure that you and the other party stick to them throughout the entire process

- Use effective communication skills including positive body language

- Prepare for compromise

- Strive for mutually beneficial solutions

- Consider whether you should seek legal advice

- Ask plenty of questions
- Pay attention to detail
- Put things in writing

Strategies for Negotiating

Understanding the other party's interests and tactics is integral to good negotiating. Choosing a strategy that best responds to the interests and tactics will help you achieve the best outcome.

Matching the Strategy to the Situation

Some of the different strategies for negotiation include"

- **Problem solving**—both parties committing to examining and discussing issues closely when entering into long-term agreements that warrant careful scrutiny

- **Contending**—persuading your negotiating party to concede to your outcome if you're bargaining in one-off negotiations or over major "wins"

- **Yielding**—conceding a point that is not vital to you that is important to the other party; valuable and ongoing negotiations

- **Compromising**—both parties forgoing their ideal outcomes, settling for an outcome that is moderately satisfactory to each participant

- **Inaction**—buying time to think about the proposal, gather more information or decide your next tactics

Your chosen strategy will depend on who you are negotiating with and the type of relationship you have with them. For example, what level of cooperation and common interest exists between you, and how will each party behave during the negotiation? It will also depend on what you are negotiating, and the timeframe and setting your negotiating in.

How to Approach a Negotiation

As well as choosing a strategy, you may wish to consider your approach to the issue being negotiated. There are three key approaches to negotiations: hard, soft, and principled negotiation. Many experts consider the third option—principled negotiation—to be the best practice:

- The hard approach involves contending by using extremely competitive bargaining.
- The soft approach involves a yielding, where one party tries hard to meet the interests of the other party and forgoes their own interests.
- Principled negotiation focuses on achieving a lasting, win-win outcome by:
    - Separating the people from the problem
    - Focusing on interests not positions
    - Generating a variety of options, before settling on an agreement
    - Basing the agreement on objective criteria

Closing of the Negotiation

Take a moment to revisit your objectives for the negotiation. Once you feel you are approaching an outcome that is acceptable to you:
- Look for closing signals; for example
    - Fading counter-arguments
    - Tired body language from the other party
    - Negotiating positions converging
- Articulate agreements and concessions already made
- Make "closing" statements; for example
    - "That suggestion might work."
    - "Right. Where do I sign?"

- Get agreements in writing as soon as you can

- Follow up promptly on any commitments you have made

Also Consider. . .

- Find out how to benchmark your business

- Your business association may provide guidance and support

When Negotiations Fail

Even with the best preparation, you may not always be able to negotiate a successful outcome. You must plan for what to do in case negotiations fail. If you allocate time and resources to planning alternative solutions, you can avoid unnecessary stress and poor business outcomes. Having an alternative plan will help you to:

- Reduce your own internal pressures

- Minimize your chances of accepting an offer that is not in your best business interests

- Set realistic goals and expectations

Preparing an Alternative Plan

It is important to remember that, when it comes to negotiating, there is always more than one positive solution for your business. Ensure you have an alternative plan.

Consider your "best alternative to a negotiated agreement" (also known as BATNA). Take pressure off yourself by identifying several other options or alternatives to the outcome you are seeking.

1. Brainstorm all available alternatives to the process you are negotiating

2. Choose the most promising ideas and expand them into practicable alternatives

3. Keep the best alternative in reserve as a fallback

Take a firm and assertive stance when proposing ideas or drawing definite lines in your negotiation. Being willing to walk away is a powerful tool.

The Negotiation Process

Every time you negotiate, you have to make choices that affect whether or not you achieve a successful outcome for your business. To get the best outcomes, you need to understand the steps involved in the negotiation process.

While many negotiations are straightforward, some will be among the hardest challenges you face. Your success will depend on planning and preparation. Always approach negotiations with a clear set of strategies, messages and tactics that can guide you from planning to closing.

Planning Your Negotiation

No amount of preparation is too much in approaching complex or high-stakes negotiations. Plan both your approach to the subject under negotiation, and your tone and communication style.
In approaching this subject of your negotiations:

- Set your objectives clearly in your own mind (including your minimum acceptable outcome, your anticipated outcome and your ideal outcome)

- Determine what you will do if the negotiation, or a particular outcome, fails

- Determine your needs, the needs of the other party and the reasons behind them

- List, rank and value your issues (and then consider concessions you might make)

- Analyze the other party (including their objectives and the information they need)

- Conduct research and consult with colleagues and partners

- Rehearse the negotiation

- Write an agenda—discussion topics, participants, location and schedule

In deciding your communication style, familiarize yourself with successful negotiating strategies. Arm yourself with a calm, confident tone and a set of considered responses and strategies to the tactics you anticipate.

Engaging with the Other Party During the Negotiation

- Introduce yourself and articulate the agenda. Demonstrate calm confidence.
- Propose—make your first offer. The other party will also make proposals. You should rarely accept their first offer. Evidence suggests that people who take the first proposal are less satisfied and regret their haste.
- Check your understanding of the other party's proposal.
- Remember your objectives.
- Discuss concepts and ideas.
- Consider appropriate compromises, then make and seek concessions.
- Suggest alternative proposals and listen to offered suggestions.
- Paraphrase others suggestions to clarify and acknowledge proposals.
- Give and take.

Consider Mediation

If negotiations are unsuccessful, be prepared to consider dispute resolution. Third-party mediation can establish a constructive environment for negotiation that requires both parties to discuss, propose and resolve issues fairly and objectively.

Conflict Resolution

Any discussion centered on negotiation must include some dwelling on the topic of conflict resolution. Conflict resolution is unfortunately an ability that leaders need to embrace, think about, and gain experience in.

When I first learned that high school curricula today includes sessions on conflict resolution, I became bemused and nostalgic. I am a child of the 1950s. Everything we ever needed to know in life about management, getting along, negotiating disputes, and conflict resolution we learned during our neighborhood "pick up" games. Every day we gathered, chose captains and then teams, and played whatever game the season of the year dictated. There were no uniforms, no coaches, no referees, no marked fields, and no hollering parents—just us and our love of the game.

Baseball was king and we played by a very complex set of practices and traditions because rarely were there enough players to fill the field. Disputes occurred often. The universal system of resolve that was employed, if discussion would not suffice, was to "shoot it out." This was our agreed go-to method to settle the argument and get back to playing. It was our system. Immediately the two parties would agree if they were going to shoot once or do a best two out of three. Then each participant declared that he took "odds" or "evens." At this point, the two placed one of their hands behind their backs and together they said "once, twice, shoot." At "shoot" each person thrust his hand in front of him with either one or two fingers out. If both players had the same number of fingers out it was even. . . and for a different number of fingers, it was odd. The winner of the shootout was awarded the positive resolve of his side of the dispute.

Another vital learning experience revolved around equipment

and borrowing. Good equipment was in short supply—especially good bats. They were all wooden at the time and were often cracked or slightly splintered. Kids became really skilled at putting screws into the cracks; never do I remember a bat being thrown away. The banter for the process of borrowing a bat went something like this. "Hey man can I borrow your bat?" "Okay, but I have chips" (chips was another word for dollars). "How many chips do you want?" "Three." "Three—it is not worth three." "Good, then don't use it." "How about two?" "No, I just repaired it." "How about two fifty?" "Okay." "Deal." "Deal."—Negotiating 101!

The successful resolution of conflict between parties relies heavily on the establishment of those parties agreeing to negotiate and for each to yield enough to where they can feel satisfied with their agreement. Leaders often facilitate and lead these proceedings.

As with most leaders, the model for my negotiating style evolved from my personality. I felt I was not capable of being effective because I'm not aggressive and "tough" enough. I abhor conflict! I was very heartened and encouraged in the early 2000s to hear of the work of Ron Shapiro, for I could easily relate to his style. His success is legendary. Mr. Shapiro authored *The Power of Nice*. In it, he espouses his life-guiding philosophy and personal value system—kindness and dedication to achieving win-win agreements. In one sentence his *Power of Nice* reads as "the best way to get what you want is to help the other side get what they want." I would note this thought as the "golden rule" of negotiating.

In the May/June issue of *Arrive Magazine*, Jon Bowen shares some further insights into Shapiro's wonderfully unorthodox, counterintuitive thinking. Bowen explains that Shapiro stresses what you need to find out before negotiating—what the other party wants out of the deal. You must therefore do research, collect information, and learn everything you can about that party's needs. He adds that you must put yourself in the other person's shoes, look for common ground.

Shapiro states: "You need two things: a philosophy and a systematic approach, a systematic approach is what empowers you."

The systematic approach has three major emphases: prepare, probe, and propose. Being prepared allows you to confidently gain control of the proceedings. Probing enables you to obtain more information (i.e., spend less time talking and more time listening and learning). In expanding upon proposing, Shapiro suggests that it be strong, solid, and reasonable. You also need to have established in your own mind when you will be prepared to walk away.

In the past few years Mr. Shapiro has written other books whose titles alone should intrigue and stir further interest. *Perfecting Your Pitch—How to Succeed in Business and in Life by Finding Words That Work;* and *Dare to Prepare—How to Win Before You Begin;* and *Bullies and Tyrants and Impossible People—How to Beat Them Without Joining Them.*

Know of, and consider, availing yourself of the training offered by the Shapiro Negotiations Institute (SNI).

Six Steps to Conflict Resolution in the Workplace

- CLARIFY WHAT THE DISAGREEMENT IS. Clarifying involves getting to the heart of the conflict. The goal of this step is to get both sides to agree on what the disagreement is. To do this, you need to discuss what needs are not being met on both sides of the conflict and ensure mutual understanding. During the process, obtain as much information as possible on each side's point of view. Continue to ask questions until you are certain that all parties involved (you and those on either side of the conflict) understand the issue.

- ESTABLISH A COMMON GOAL FOR BOTH PARTIES. In this step of the process, both sides agree on the desired outcome of the conflict. "When people know that they're working towards the same goal, then they're more apt to participate truthfully to make sure that they reach that end goal together." Kimberly A. Benjamin explained in a recent BLR webinar. To accomplish this, discuss what each party would like to see happen and find a commonality in both sides as a starting point for a shared outcome. That commonality can be as simple as "both sides want to end the conflict."

- DISCUSS WAYS TO MEET THE COMMON GOAL. This involves listening, communicating, and brainstorming together. Continue with both sides working together to discuss ways that they can meet that goal they agreed on in step 2. Keep going until all the options are exhausted.

- DETERMINE THE BARRIERS TO THE COMMON GOAL. In this step of the process, the two parties acknowledge what has brought them into the conflict and talk about what problems may prevent a resolution. Understanding the possible problems that may be encountered along the way lets you proactively find solutions that have plans in place to handle issues. Define what can and cannot be changed about the situation. For the items that cannot be changed, discuss ways of getting around those road blocks.

- AGREE ON THE BEST WAY TO RESOLVE THE CONFLICT. Both parties need to come to a conclusion on the best resolution. Start by identifying solutions that both sides can live with. Ask both sides and see where there is common ground. Then start to discuss the responsibility each party has in maintaining the solution. It is also important to use opportunity to get to the root cause to ensure this conflict will not come up again. "A lot of times when we try to fix problems, we get so caught up in fixing it that we do not identify what we need to do so it doesn't happen," Benjamin cautioned.

- ACKNOWLEDGE THE AGREED UPON SOLUTION AND DETERMINE THE RESPONSIBILITIES EACH PARTY HAS IN THE RESOLUTION. Both sides need to own their responsibility in the resolution of the conflict and express aloud what they have agreed to. After both parties have acknowledged a win-win situation, ask both parties to use phrases such as "I agree to. . . " and "I acknowledge that I have responsibility for. . . "

The most intense negotiation I have ever been involved in was the sale of the Bagel Chip company to Nabisco; talk about David and Goliath!

The entire process took almost eight months to complete. There was a myriad of organizational and logistical issues that rendered a fairly straightforward deal into one that became cumbersome and complex.

Two episodes stand out in my mind, that, upon reflection, confirm that you can be your honest self and succeed in coming to terms and making the deal happen.

The final discussions were held over a two-week period in all-day sessions on a Thursday and Friday and then again, the next Thursday and Friday—with the goal of closing the deal at 9:00am on the second Friday. These meetings were held in the Corporate Board Room of Nabisco, Inc., in New York City.

I have a wonderful memory of sitting across the table from about five vice presidents trying desperately to answer their inquiries as I gazed out at the Empire State Building! I literally pinched myself in recognition of the unlikeliness of me ever being in this position again. It was surreal.

At about 11:00pm on the second Thursday, when everyone was exhausted, a vice president from Nabisco asked if we had "stack permits" for our ovens. I answered, "No." He then told me and the group that he was very uncomfortable going through with the deal "if there is an E.P.A. issue." I was mortified. Further discussion revealed that about a year earlier, New Jersey had passed legislation that large stacks needed to be tested and adjudicated to be in compliance for certain emission requirements. I had no knowledge of this.

After a brief period of reflection and a side bar with my attorney, I offered the group an apology for our oversight of this issue but encouraged them not to quell the proceedings but rather to accept a resolve whereby we would escrow $200,000; only to be re-paid upon our presentation of the appropriate permits in their names. I assured them I could accomplish this in one month.

I was relieved and pleased when the vice president agreed saying, "Your word is good enough for me; and so is the money!"

As I was sighing in relief and packing up, Nabisco's lead attorney asked if he could have a moment with me. With brevity he explained to me that the table had forty-six piles, one for each document that needed to be signed. Unfortunately, one of the piles could not be signed and distributed because a lease release document for trucks we were leasing in Chicago had not been received. It was one of my responsibilities to get that signed. I quickly assured him that if I had to drive to Chicago over the weekend, it wiould be signed by Monday morning and on his desk. He said, "I trust you," and walked away.

The next morning, I walked into the board room and the signing commenced. I was the only person to count the piles. There were forty-five; one pile had disappeared!

The gavel came down. "Bam!" We had a deal. Whew!

Upon reflection, I realize that you have to be patient when negotiating. Take advantage of any time and opportunity that allows you to portray your values and your willingness to be conciliatory. People need to sense your commitment to honoring your word. They need to trust you. This is the fuel that allows the proceedings to ultimately render a conclusion that results in true collaboration.

O

"O"
is for
"Organization"

Organization

Being organized, and enjoying a sense of confidence that you are indeed orgainzed, is of inestimable benefit to entrepreneurial-minded leaders. Organization is the fundamental tool by which you steward your greatest asset—time.

Dr. Randy Pausch, a beloved professor from Carnegie Mellon University in Pittsburgh, authored a book entitled *The Last Lecture* while battling pancreatic cancer. He was forty-seven years old when he passed away. This powerful work is a very moving and thought-provoking read. Randy's main thesis was expounded in his words: "*Time* is your greatest gift—you never know how much you have; use it wisely."

By maintaining our possessions, activities, and environments in good order, we enhance well-being and our sense of organization and control. By so doing and living, we are more efficient, and thus better able to steward the gift of time.

"Knowing that what you are doing is the most important thing for you to be doing at that moment is surprisingly powerful."—Daniel J. Leviton

"With a place for everything, and everything in its place" mindset and routine, we minimize time spent wastefully as we embark and engage in our tasks and efforts. We are better prepared when organized; this makes us economical in our efforts and contributes to our goal of being calm and content.

Organization reduces "do overs"—having to repeat the work. As the old adage goes, "If you do not take the time to do it right the first time, how will you ever find the time to do it again?"

When you are an organized leader, it is obvious and impactful to others. People can witness organization in everything—from your dress and your workspace to your speech and your deportment. It cultivates a way of living and thinking among the persons following you. Others will emulate your example and it will benefit them and your organization, with everyone striving for orderliness and control.

Orderliness makes the impression (especially the first one) on others that an establishment that appears as such is worthy of their enterprise and that the experience will be profitable. Clutter, on the other hand, is the enemy of visual calm and quiet. It literally lowers your influence and mood and is not a pleasant place to be or deal with.

Organization should, and is, receiving much attention from psychologists and other scientists. I bring to your attention, for example, an insightful read called *The Organized Mind—Thinking Straight in the Age of Information Overload* by Daniel J. Leviton. Mr. Leviton states: "No other species lives with regret over past events, or makes deliberate plans for future ones." He continues, "The most fundamental principle of the organized mind, the one most crucial to keeping us from forgetting or losing things, is to shift the burden of organizing from our brains to the external world."

There are probably as many systems and strategies for being organized as there are the number of leaders employing them! Everyone has his means towards the end. Some reflections on a few common denominators of these models and some suggested readings and tools might aid in your organizing plans and efforts.

Take Notes

The most dominant trait and habitual activity I note in organized leaders is that they are obsessive about taking notes and writing things down. I would call this effort "memorializing." We only retain 20 percent of what we hear. Writing is helpful in retention now and more importantly later. Journaling is a means for retrieval when needed and notes can be disseminated easily to all the other parties that need to be "on the same page"—literally! I find that the very act of writing provides a prompt to my ability to recall. It helps make the note indelible and concrete. Writing therefore stimulates your attention and contemplation regarding the subject you are writing about. By putting things in writing, and asking others to do the same, leaders incorporate into their organization a heightened state of accountability for people to read, digest, and, in turn, act upon what others write to them and what they write to others.

Checklists

In a very compelling and practical book entitled *Checklist Manifesto* by Dr. Atul Gawande, one learns how to appreciate and utilize checklists in organizing daily and professional life. This book examines the use of checklists in current medical practice and procedure and reflects on its use in organizing and preparing activities. Know that Dr. Gawande's study was prompted after reading a story about a young child who survived a fall into a frozen pond and his discovering that the physician who saved her life relied heavily on the use of a checklist.

Checklists are tools that, via the documentation they demand, and attention to a sequential list thus assuring compliance and completion, insure adherence. Even a single unchecked box in essence indicates failure and calls for renewed focus. It is therefore an invaluable tool for preparation, execution, and providing evidence of execution. Gawande shares his obvious excitement about the use of checklists in medicine, but his learning and writing is applicable to every imaginable effort or initiative people engage in when they desire to be thorough, responsible, and unequivocally organized.

Charts and Graphs

The integration of technology into your organizing efforts can be of valuable assistance and benefit. The goal is to always efficiently be able to recover the information that was stored.

The growth of virtual meetings is especially beneficial when you are employing PERT charts or flow charts into your organizational model.

A basic flowchart for organizing is provided at this link; please study it.[12]

---

12 https://support.microsoft.com/en-us/office/create-a-basic-flowchart-in-visio-e207d975-4a51-4bfa-a356-eeec314bd276

A flowchart is the type of diagram that represents a workflow or process. A flowchart can also be defined as a diagrammatic representation of an algorithm—a step-by-step approach for solving a task.

Many software packages exist that can create flowcharts readily, either directly for programming language source code, or from a flowchart description language.

PERT charts (Program Evaluation and Review Technique) are statistical tools developed by the United States Navy in 1958 and are often used in conjunction with the Critical Path Method (CPM). A PERT chart is a project management tool used to schedule, organize, and coordinate tasks within a project. It is basically a method to analyze the individual task in completing a given project; especially noting the time to complete the task; and to identify the minimum time to complete the entire project. All measure of additional data such as resources required and the person(s) responsible can be recorded and tracked.

To further familiarize yourself as to the benefits of PERT charts; particularly when projects are complex, with many persons, over an extended tenure, please avail yourself of the websites. Monday.com; Smartsheet.com or a Gantt Chart.

The next few pages are an example of a PERT chart employed by a group moving a factory from one country to another. A book could be written if one were to write all the information that could be drawn from these charts. Also pay particular attention to the email that instructs the team regarding an upcoming meeting. It demonstrates the efficiency of the employment of these forms of data collection, dissemination, and how they are now of even greater aid with the integration of technology. Recording responsible parties and dates is key to clarity and accountability.

Team

In order to keep the meeting efficient and best utilize everyone's collaborative time wisely, please observe and respect the following requests:

- Each task within the schedule has been assigned to a specific person(s); this person(s) will be responsible for active updates of his/her assigned task(s) within the document

- This includes but is not limited to making adjustments

- Please be sure to log into the schedule frequently throughout the week to keep your assigned tasks up to date with the latest information on an ongoing basis

- Please ensure that all of your assigned tasks are updated within the schedule prior to the start of every meeting

- Please come to each meeting prepared to speak about your assigned opened tasks in a clear/concise manner

- Deep discussions and decisions are to be made outside of this meeting, to be organized and led by the appropriate staff and involve appropriate parties.

Final Suggestions

At a more practical level, consider some suggestions that I have employed and some that I have observed work for others. If there are activities or conversations on your agenda that you are uncomfortable about or anxious over, attempt to schedule them to be tackled first thing in your day and get them behind you. They are mentally taxing and distracting. Completing them will relax you and allow you to focus more ably on the next item on your agenda.

A structured routine and schedule can benefit you and those who engage with you. An example of this might be that you set aside two times a day to review and respond to emails. Dutifully see to it that you adhere to the schedule and share this with your colleagues. You will find, in time, that people will accommodate your schedule and will appreciate it because you respond in a focused frame of mind, and are more thorough and succinct. Fighting the tyranny of the urgent and constantly having to put out fires robs a leader of the ability to work and think with a clear, calm mind. Haste makes waste as we know.

We all need to exercise initiative and discipline to control and organize every domain of our lives. We aim to be pleasantly obsessive! By so doing, we shepherd time, create pleasant and efficient environments to live and work in, and enjoy a sense of peace in a quieter mind and with a confident demeanor.

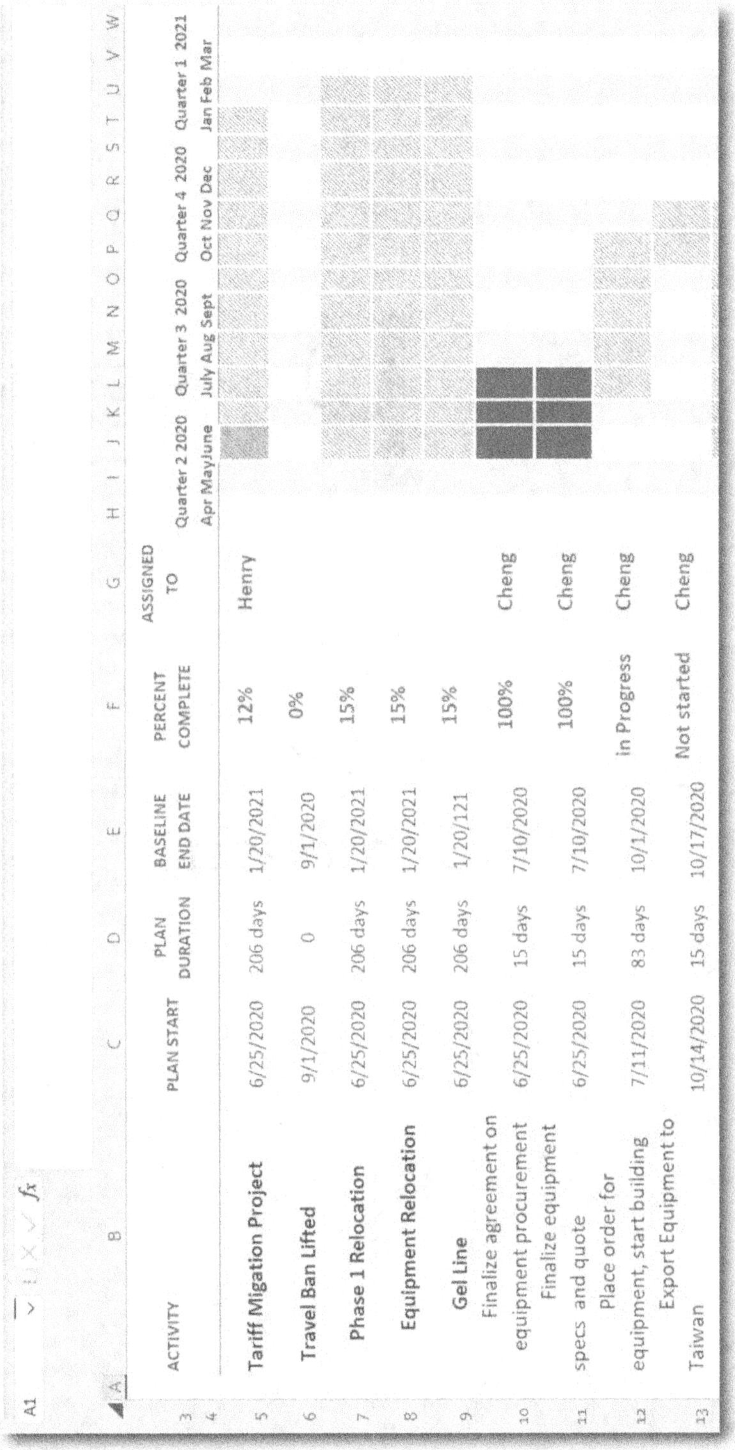

ACTIVITY	PLAN START	PLAN DURATION	BASELINE END DATE	PERCENT COMPLETE	ASSIGNED TO	Quarter 2 2020 Apr May June	Quarter 3 2020 July Aug Sept	Quarter 4 2020 Oct Nov Dec	Quarter 1 2021 Jan Feb Mar
Tariff Migation Project	6/25/2020	206 days	1/20/2021	12%	Henry				
Travel Ban Lifted	9/1/2020	0	9/1/2020	0%					
Phase 1 Relocation	6/25/2020	206 days	1/20/2021	15%					
Equipment Relocation	6/25/2020	206 days	1/20/2021	15%					
Gel Line	6/25/2020	206 days	1/20/121	15%					
Finalize agreement on equipment procurement	6/25/2020	15 days	7/10/2020	100%	Cheng				
Finalize equipment specs and quote	6/25/2020	15 days	7/10/2020	100%	Cheng				
Place order for equipment, start building	7/11/2020	83 days	10/1/2020	in Progress	Cheng				
Export Equipment to Taiwan	10/14/2020	15 days	10/17/2020	Not started	Cheng				

P

"P"
is for
"Preparation"

Preparation—Preparedness

The motto which all Boy Scouts strive to uphold is "Be Prepared." This is a fine mantra for leaders and all of us as well. Scouts are trained to be prepared in mind by having disciplined themselves to be obedient to every order, and also by having thought out beforehand any accident or situation that might occur so that they know the right thing to do at the right moment, and are *willing* to do it. "Always be ready to do your duty," is a key saying from the Boy Scout handbook.

The Roman philosopher Seneca stated: "We make our own luck; luck is opportunity meeting up with preparation, so you must prepare yourself to be lucky."

Louis Pasteur, the renowned French scientist who developed the principles of vaccination and pasteurization, remarked, "Chance favors the prepared mind."

Former United States President General Dwight D. Eisenhower, who planned the D-Day landing in France during World War II, made some penetrating observations: "Preparing for battle I have always found that plans are worthless, but planning is indispensable." He also said, "Planning for an emergency you must start with this one thing: the very definition of 'emergency' is that it is unexpected, therefore, it is not going to happen the way you are planning."

Preparing and planning is an ongoing—even relentless—task of a leader. Expecting the unexpected (and being ready and willing to tackle it when it comes) is a must.

In practical terms, preparedness is seeing to it that you have contemplated possible future events and have gathered the resources together that you need to effectuate your plan—within the established schedule. I once learned that leaders or managers should think of themselves as a COP. Their main function is to Control, Organize and Plan.

I acknowledge that, in a small business, it is difficult enough for you to attend to the daily affairs let alone find extra time to devote to preparing for possible problems, but you must.

Single Point of Failure

My experience has taught me that a strategy to efficiently identify, and develop preparedness for, is to first seek out situations that could be declared a single point of failure. The dictionary's definition of a single point of failure is "a potential risk posed by a flaw in the design, implementation, or configuration of a circuit or system in which one fault or malfunction causes an entire system to stop operating, in other words, if one thing breaks it all goes down."[13]

In plain words, you are up the creek without a paddle!

The most obvious remedy is to have redundancy (i.e., a spare or an extra of that which, if it fails, you can quickly repair or replace it). This is the case with machines and software, etc., but the expense often prohibits having two in your possession. Some practical policies such as having a spare parts inventory, a robust preventative maintenance program, and strong working relationships with technicians are advisable to thwart down time.

Another common point of failure regards a valuable employee who performs specialized functions. If that person is absent, for any reason, then that function does not get accomplished.

Here again the obvious solution is to always have a two-deep person competency for each critical position in the company, (i.e., people cross trained). In a small business, this is a luxury rarely enjoyed because people do not have the time to train or to be trained on a second task as they are already stretched performing their primary responsibilities. There is a natural reticence in most people to train others to do their job. They worry they will be replaced. A leader must propose and employ an each-one-teach-one philosophy and spirit. Demonstrate to your people that you strive to advance people into new and better jobs from your current ranks before hiring someone new from the outside. This will educate and

13   Tech Target 8/31/2018

ensure people that they need to "train their replacement" or they cannot move up and forward.

As a leader you need to speak of and demonstrate your adherence to practices that are trustworthy.

One proven method of exposing and training people in new assignments is to have them shadow or follow the trainer for a period of time and then gradually perform tasks under the watchful eye of the trainer. It is basically mentoring. It can be very effective.

Preparation Strategies

The Leaders Checklist—quoted below—is Michael Useems' checklist as written in his book. It is a thorough list of questions to aid leaders in their ongoing preparedness. He writes: "The Leaders Checklist is meant to serve as a trigger to leadership action. Individually, though, each principle should generate a set of questions that will help leaders test, retest, refine, and update their preparedness for almost any situation." Here are some prompts for each of the precepts:

1. Articulate a Vision

- Do my direct reports see the forest, not just the trees?

- Does everyone in the firm know not only where we are going, but why?

- Is the destination compelling and appealing?

2. Think and Act Strategically

- Do we have a realistic plan both for creating a short-term result and for mapping out the future?

- Have you considered all the players and anticipated every roadblock?

- Has everybody embraced—and can everybody explain—the firm's competitive strategy and value drivers?

3. Honor the Room

- Do those in the room know that you respect and value their talents and efforts?

- Have you made it clear that their upward guidance is always sought?
- Is there a sense of engagement on the front lines, and do they see themselves as "us," not "them"?

4. Take Charge

- Are you prepared to take charge even when you are not in charge?
- If so, do you, with a capacity and position to embrace responsibility?
- For the technical decisions ahead, are you ready to delegate but not abdicate?

5. Act Decisively

- Are most of your decisions both good and timely?
- Do you convey your strategic intent and then let others reach their own decisions?
- Is your own decision threshold close to a "70 percent" go point?

6. Communicate Persuasively

- Are the messages about vision, strategy, and character crystal-clear and indelible?
- Have you mobilized all communication channels, from purely personal to social media?
- Can you deliver a compelling speech before the elevator passes the tenth floor?

7. Motivate the Troops

- Have you identified each person's "hot button" and focused on it?
- Do you work personal pride and shared purpose into most communications?
- Are you keeping some ammunition dry for urgent moments when you need it?

8. Embrace the Front Lines

- Have you made your intent clear and empowered those around you to act?

- Do you regularly meet with those in direct contact with customers?

- Is everybody able to communicate their ideas and concerns to you?

9. Build Leadership in Others

- Are all managers expected to build leadership among their subordinates?

- Does the company culture foster the effective exercise of leadership?

- Are leadership development opportunities available to most, if not all, managers?

10. Mandate Relations

- Is the hierarchy reduced to a minimum, and does bad news travels up?

- Are managers self-aware and empathetic?

- Are autocratic, egocentric, and irritable behaviors censored?

11. Identify Personal Implications

- Do employees appreciate how the firm's vision and strategy impact them individually?

- What private sacrifices will be necessary for achieving the common cause?

- How will the plan affect people's personal livelihood and quality of work life?

12. Convey your Character

- Have you communicated your commitment to performance with integrity?

- Do those in the organization know you as a person, and do

they know your aspirations and your hopes?

- Have you been in the same room with everybody who works with you within the past year?

13. Dampen Over-Optimism

- Have you prepared the organization for unlikely but extremely consequential events?
- Do you celebrate success but also guard against the by-product of excess confidence?
- Have you paved the way not only for quarterly results but for long-term performance?

14. Build a Diverse Top Team

- Have you drawn quality performers into your inner circle?
- Are they diverse in expertise but united in purpose?
- Are they as engaged and energized as you?

15. Place Common Interest First

- In all decisions, have you placed shared purpose ahead of private gain?
- Do the firm's vision and strategy embody the organization's mission?
- Are you thinking like a president or chief executive even if you're not one?

159

Q

"Q"

is for

"Question"

Question

Entrepreneurial leaders are the most inquisitive and persistent people you will ever have the pleasure to encounter! By nature, it seems, they tend to be incessantly striving to understand and gain knowledge; they are interested and curious about everything and everybody. They invite and relish discourse and conversation.

Leaders are quick studies and good listeners. They are attentive to what is happening around them and aware of whose presence they are in. They are accumulators of knowledge and information they sense might aid them in their ventures. Leaders are vacuums, always taking in new material!

Effective people "connect dots"; they look for and study the interplay, the connections, the trends, the patterns, similarities, common denominators, and cause-and-effect phenomena of all manner of circumstances and situations. Nothing is taken for granted or at face value. They search beyond the obvious and seek motive and reason.

Entrepreneurial leaders are on a constant quest of examining and explaining the confluence of things, the interweaving of things, and all forms of enterprise and initiative.

Leaders muse and think, deduce, and intuit to form their opinions, perspective, decisions, judgments, and paths forward.

I observe that most leaders are proficient and rabid readers. Theodore Roosevelt said, "I am a part of everything I have read." Charles T. Jones offered this comment: "You will be the same person in five years except for the people you meet and the books you have read."

Entrepreneurial leaders will not read over a word they do not know and then not take a moment to look it up. Think about how many times you learn a new word and, in as little as a day or two, there it is again! Knowledge is so valuable and always worth the effort.

Adam Bryant writes a weekly column for the *New York Times*. He wrote an article on October 17, 2017, entitled: "How to be a CEO" taken from a decade's worth of his collection of work. These are his reflections and some others he shares in his article.

Passionate Curiosity

Many successful chief executives are passionately curious people. It is a side of them rarely seen in the media and in investor meetings, and there is a reason for that. In business, CEOs are supposed to project confidence in breezy authority as they take an audience through their projections of steady growth. Certainty is a game face they wear. They've cracked the code.

But to get them away from these familiar scripts, a different side emerges. They share stories about failures and doubts and mistakes. They ask big-picture questions. They wonder why things work the way they do and whether those things can be improved upon. They want to know people's stories, and what they do.

It's this relentless questioning that leads entrepreneurs to spot new opportunities and helps managers understand the people who work with them, and how to get them to work together effectively. It is no coincidence that more than one executive uttered the same phrase when describing what, ultimately, is the CEO's job: "I am a student of human nature."

The C.E.O.s are not necessarily the smartest people in the room, but they are the best students—the letters could just as easily stand for "chief education officer."

"You learn from everybody," said Alan R. Mulally, the chief executive of the Ford Motor Company. "I've always just wanted to learn everything, to understand anybody that I was around—why they thought what they did, why they did what they did, what worked for them, what didn't work."

Why "passionate curiosity"? The phrase is more than the sum of its parts, which individually fall short in capturing the quality that sets these CEO's apart. There are plenty of people who are passionate, but many of their passions are focused on just one area. There are a lot of curious people in the world, but they can also be wallflowers.

But "passionate curiosity"—a phrase used by Nell Minow, the co-founder of the Corporate Library—better captures the infectious sense of fascination that some people have with everything around them.

"Passionate curiosity," Ms. Minow said, "is indispensable, no matter what the job is. You want somebody who is just alert and very awake and engaged with the world and wanting to know more."

Though chief executives are paid to have the answers, their greatest contributions to their organizations may be asking the right questions. They recognize that they can't have the answer to everything, but they can push their company in new directions and marshal the collective energy of their employees by asking the right questions.

"In business, the big prizes are found when you can ask a question that challenges the corporate orthodoxy," said Andrew Cosslett, the CEO of the Intercontinental Hotels Group. "In every business I worked in, there's been a lot of cost and value locked up in things that are deemed to be 'the way we do things around here.' So you have to talk to people and ask them, 'Why do you do that?'"

It's an important lesson. For all the furrowed-brow seriousness that you often encounter in the business world, some of the most important advances come from asking, much like a persistent five-year-old, the simplest questions. "Why do you do that? How come it's done this way? Is there a better way?"

R

"R"
is for
"Risk"

Risk

Risk—Definitely; Reward—Maybe!

Behold the turtle who never gets anywhere until he sticks his neck out!

It has always intrigued me and inspired me that so many men and women are willing to choose an entrepreneurial, leadership life. The odds are heavily against them, but they forge on.

By choosing such a path, one risks time, money, comfort, stability, and—most significantly—failure; and its potential social stigma and embarrassment. Therefore, sacrifice of "self" is the most daunting requirement of this path.

Respected Christian author and church developer, Tim Keller, acknowledges that entrepreneurial leaders "[w]ant to create space to do good. In essence these creators want to show and practice love; not for power and money per se but to contribute, sacrifice and share." But, he warns, there is "tremendous cost and risk."

Through primarily the thoughtful words of others, my intent in this chapter is to encourage, embolden, and inspire your ambition. May you find these musings motivating. I sincerely and prayerfully hope that you will follow the call you hear and feel it in your heart.

"If our principles are right, why should we be cowards?"
— Lilli De Jong

"You may be disappointed if you fail, but you're doomed if you don't try."
—Opera great, Beverly Sills

"Only those who risk going too far will ever know how far they can go."

Show me a person who makes no mistakes and never fails, and I will show you a person who does not do anything.

"Expect difficulties, strain and suffering. It takes three times as long and costs three times more than your estimate."
—Karen Horbett

"You will never be the person you can be if pressures, tension, and disciplines are taken out of your life."
—Christian scholar C.S. Lewis

"One of the stepping stones of life is to make stepping stones of stumbling blocks."
—Jack Penn

An entrepreneur is an over-comer.

"The greatest risk of pursuing a leadership opportunity is that you expose yourself and become vulnerable and open to others. The times can be uncomfortable. The only antidote is courage, conviction, and confidence. Just know that most will not even think about subjecting themselves to these potential struggles. This fact alone can be a reason to persevere and carry on! You are at least trying. 'You cannot win if you do not play.'"
—Steve Forbert

"Whatever you can do, or dream you can, begin it. Boldness has genius, power, and magic in it."
—Johann Wolfgang von Goethe

"Facing difficulties and strain are transforming—embrace them and be attentive to their benefits. Courage is very important. Like a muscle, it's strengthened by use."
—Ruth Gordon

Know that your life and work encourages others.

"That someone should be successful, shows that others may become successful, and hence, is just encouragement to industry and enterprise."
—Abraham Lincoln, paraphrased in 1864

"Courage is contagious. When a brave person takes a stand, the spines of others are stiffened."
—Evangelist Billy Graham

"After crosses and losses people grow humbler and wiser."
—Ben Franklin

"The only sure bet is to bet on yourself. It is all that you control."
—Mike Gray

FEAR:

False
Evidence
Appearing
Real

Risk and Reward[14]

A discussion regarding risk and reward, and the need to be courageous would be wanting if the notion of fear was omitted. Fear is a parasite to the will and soul of people; especially entrepreneurial leaders.

Fear is akin to fire. On a cold winter's night nothing is more pleasant than sitting in front of a fireplace enjoying its ambience and warmth. However, when uncontrolled, fire can destroy thousands of acres and homes in very short order.

Fear is defined as an unpleasant emotion caused by the belief that someone or something is dangerous, likely to cause pain or be a threat.

14 From: *Lead Like Jesus*—Ken Blanchard and Phil Hodges

Fear is an involuntary feeling. In its proper perspective it aids in guiding us to make appropriate preparations, to act safely and cautiously as we go about our activities, and it sobers our judgment as we contemplate situations that have inherent risk or can cause potential harm.

On the other hand, fear that is unchecked can distract and rob us of the ability to focus and think clearly. It can literally paralyze us and bring progress to a complete halt.

It can be difficult to achieve, but the key to minimizing fear's impact is to keep it in check or at bay to the very best you are able. One initiative that has helped me is to keep a Journal of Worry! In my journal, I take particular note of what is troubling me and what I am projecting to be an issue in the future. Periodically I look back and assess as to how many of my trepidations were warranted. Rarely, if ever, are they! The journal allows me to consider facts and truth and not waste time and energy on speculations. It is a filter or block to dissuade further thoughts about ideations or feelings of fear when they arise and distract. I strive to stay in the moment and discipline myself to see the empirical, the "know," rather than erroneous musings and conjecture.

Prime Minister Winston Churchill, who guided Great Britain through the horror and fear of the Second World War, proclaimed: "Success consists of going from failure to failure without losing enthusiasm."

"Success is not final; failure is not fatal. It is the courage to continue that counts."
—Winston Churchill

S

"S"
is for
"Success"

Success

Please take a moment and write an obituary that you would hope someone years from now would write about you:

I apologize for launching this discussion with such a profound and perhaps even morbid task, but I do so advisedly. Sometimes we have to be forced to look back and reflect so that, as we go forward, our paths are directed and purposeful and then ultimately our lives are fulfilling and fully realized.

Success is an extremely subjective state and is often distorted by mistruths and socially misguided values and whims.

At age fifty-four, I embarked on a journey that began with the dreaded word "cancer" followed by the words, "It would be best to get your affairs in order," being spoken to me. These episodes in life are always shocking and surreal but they forever change you from that moment on. Between initial diagnosis and surgery for biopsies and then the subsequent surgery I had a month to reflect. Upon the advice of a counselor, I started a journal and began to muse on his suggestion that I should think about my obituary.

My thoughts were predominantly influenced by a beautiful book I was blessed and fortunate to have read a short time before—*Halftime* by Bob Buford. The subtitle for this book is: *Moving from Success to Significance.*

Buford believes that we should take a "halftime" of sorts and assess and muse as to where we are going and why. He urges us to carefully identify what we want to do with the second half of our lives. For most of us, especially me, success equaled substance—things and money. Buford's book and the impact of my battle completely amended my thinking toward realizing that success is living a fulfilled, fruitful life—a life that is focused on relationships and striving for significance. Buford advocates correctly that using a barometer of gauging the significance of what you are about, your purpose, and what you are doing can lead to a life of joy, impact, and balance.

Success is peace of mind which is a direct result of self-satisfaction in knowing you did your best to become the best that you are capable of becoming.

John R. Wooden, Head Basketball Coach, Emeritus, UCLA

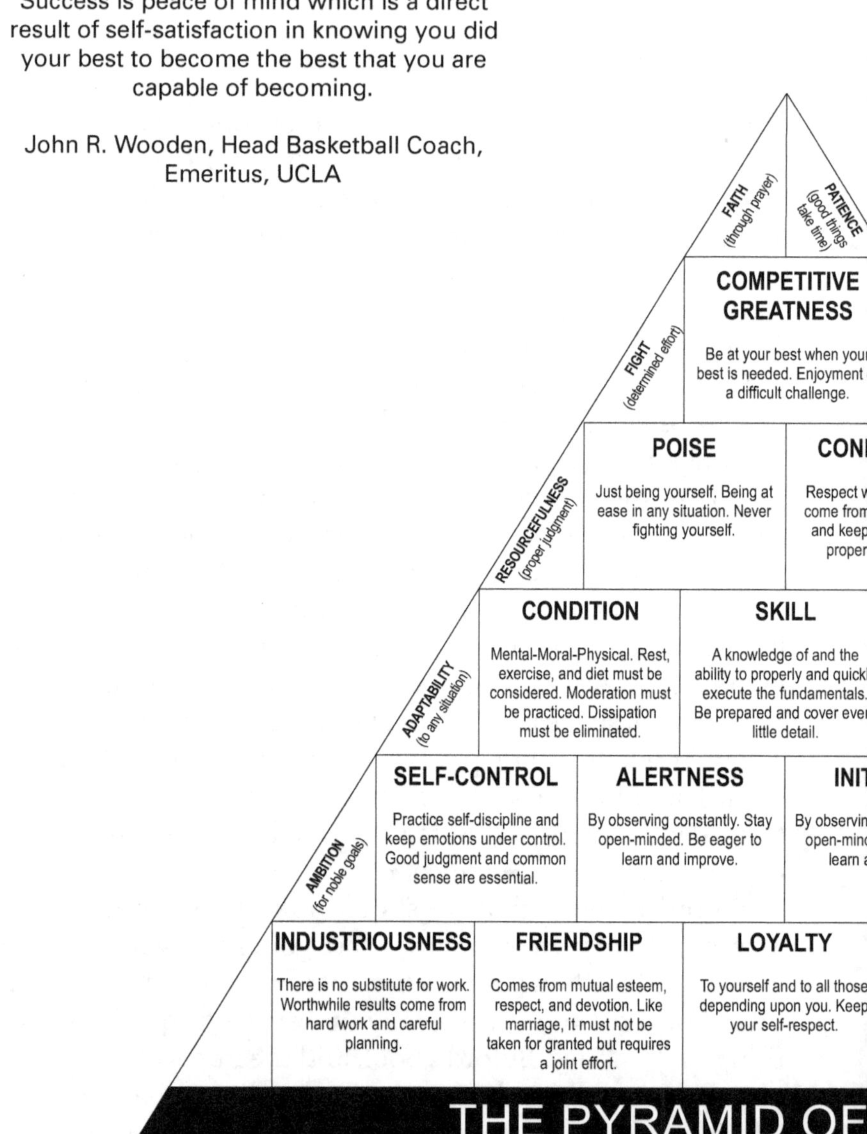

Please know that I am not saying that money is not an appropriate motivator or proper reward for risk, sacrifice, and effort, but just see that it does not become the sole focus. Your obituary will not state your net worth, but it will clearly acknowledge the worth you were to others.

Best wishes
John Wooden

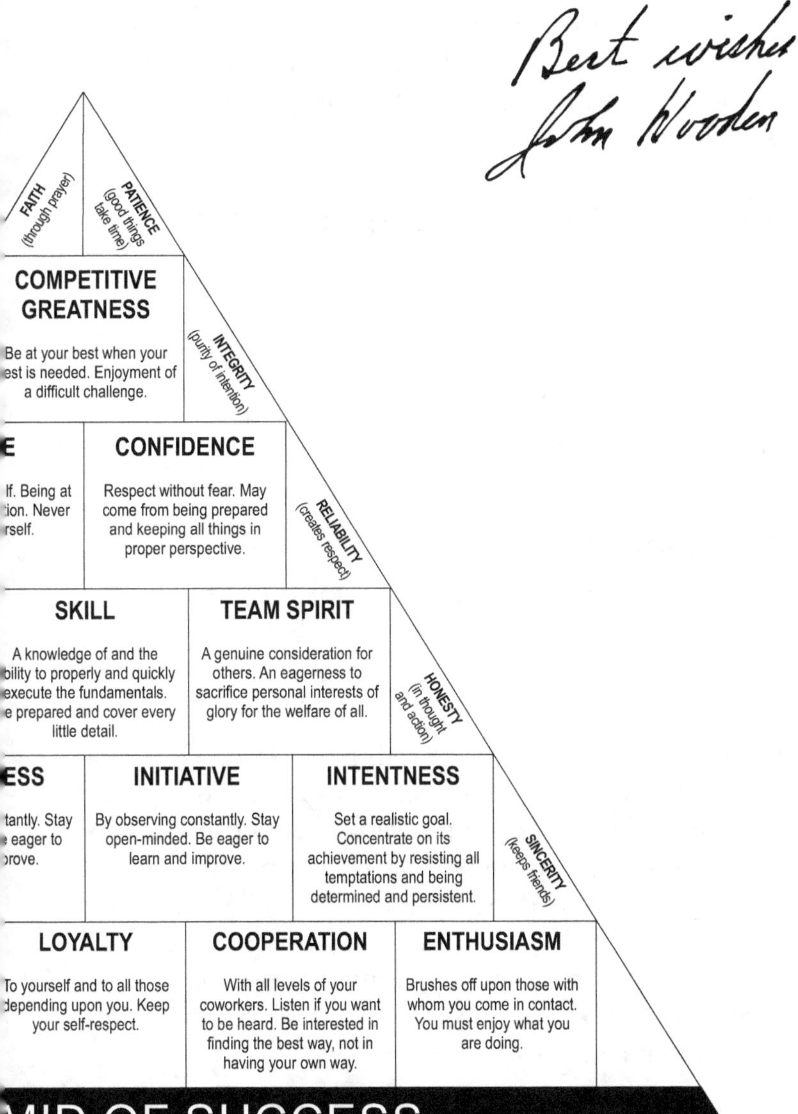

Studying the models and prerequisites for what successful people think make for success is enlightening. For instance, I have always been mindful of the "Pyramid of Success" as developed by the revered and legendary basketball coach, John Wooden, of the UCLA men's basketball team (see page 172). It is replete with inspiring thoughts and concepts as to teamwork and the constructs of success. It is thought-provoking to learn that the implementation of value and virtues is so paramount to successful efforts and results. Wooden extols the reality that character inculcates achievement. He further adds that, in the end, success is peace of mind attained by doing your best and working hard.

"Seven things to do to be successful" [15]

1. Be true to yourself;

2. Help others;

3. Make each day your masterpiece;

4. Drink deeply from good books;

5. Make friendship a fine art;

6. Build a shelter against a rainy day;

7. Seek guidance and council and give thanks for your blessings each day.

Seven habits of successful entrepreneurship by Walter Grant released in his book *Effective Entrepreneurship,* eloquently offers this in his chapter titled *Final Words*: "What separates those who are successful from those whose businesses barely get off the ground is their willingness to commit themselves to the habits, sticking to them even when it is hard, even when you think of giving up, you will become a more effective entrepreneur. Every day, you will bring yourself one step closer to success, and your commitment will more than pay for itself."

---

15 by John Wooden—from www.woodencourse.com

1. Remain persistent;

2. Keep learning;

3. Think long-term;

4. Find A- players;

5. Stay focused;

6. Structure environment;

7. Prioritize health.

"Many people view integrity as some form of duty. Integrity is not a duty. It is a means to improve the probability of being successful and happy."
—Bob Burg[16]

Success is paradoxical by nature. We assume it springs from wealth and material abundance. We learn in the end, however, that it is much more of an attitude or feeling. Feelings follow action. If you act successful (i.e., follow your principles and that to which you aspire to be), you feel successful, therefore, you are successful. For me, I need to affirm every day in my mind, that knowing I'm doing my best to live a life of purpose, with practiced virtues, honoring commitments, being generous, kind, and grateful, I am successful because I feel content.

So, follow your passion; go forth, strive for significance by being good to others and thus living well.

"Honesty and integrity are the building blocks to success."
—Bob Page

16 Bob Burg, written on 2/2/2018 in: https://www.bizjournals.com/bizjournals/how-to/growth-strategies/2018/02/how-integrity-improves-your-chances-of-being.html quoting John Allison from his book *The Leadership Crisis and The Free Market Cure.*

Success

*(These words are often attributed to
Elisabeth-Anne Anderson Stanley.)*

*Too laugh often and love much
To win the respect of intelligent people
and the affection of children*

*To earn the appreciation of honest critics
Endure the betrayal of false friends*

*To appreciate beauty
To find the best in others
To leave the world a bit better
whether by a healthy child,
A garden patch, or even deemed social condition*

*To know even one life has breathed easier
Because you have lived.
This is to have succeeded.*

The Dash Poem

By Linda Ellis

*I read of a man who stood to speak
At the funeral of a friend.
He referred to the dates on her tombstone
From the beginning to the end.*

*He noted that first came the date of her birth
And spoke of the following date with tears,
But he said what mattered most of all
Was the dash between those years.*

For that dash represents all the time
The she spent alive on earth
And only those who loved her
Know what that little line is worth.

For it matters not, how much we own,
The cars, the house, the cash,
What matters is how we live and love
And how we spend our dash

So think about this long and hard;
Are there things you'd like to change?
For you never know how much time is left
That can still be rearranged.

If we could just slow down enough
To consider what's true and real
And always try to understand
The way other people feel.

And be less quick to anger
And show appreciation more
And love the people in our lives
Like we've never loved before.

If we treat each other with respect
And more often wear a smile,
Remembering that this special dash
Might only last a little while.

So when your eulogy is being read
With your life's actions to rehash
Would you be proud of the things they say
About how you spend your dash?

This author's muse: I am convinced that people experience the truest sense of success when they are aware of—and confident that—they have aided and abetted others to achieve a sense of success and well-being.

T

"T"
is for
"Time; Talent; Treasure"

Time; Talent; Treasure

In the Bible, there are encouragements for believers to recognize and give thanks for all they have been given, to be good caretakers of this bounty, and to share it generously with those less fortunate. The recommendation is to give at least 10 percent of your time, talent, and treasure.

Creative leaders have a duty to steward their organization and the people in it but to also share themselves with their families, communities, and the world at large.

By integrating into civic life, you create some balance in your schedule and activities as well as being a benefit to others by sharing your experience and wisdom. It makes you feel whole and satisfied to do so. Through giving, you, in turn, receive the worth of feeling generous and contributing to others unselfishly.

There are volunteer-based not-for-profit operations that address every conceivable domain of need and challenge our world faces. Most of them are in constant search for Board of Director members and committee heads that would be enriched by your skills, energy, and know-how.

Religious groups have mission initiatives that address a myriad of situations and conditions in which people are suffering and in need. Much work is being done to address causes, not just symptoms.

"Give a man a fish and he eats for a day; teach a man to fish and he eats for a lifetime."

With this spirit in mind, for instance, I recently learned of a group in Salt Lake City named *Warriors Rising*. Their vision is to come alongside veterans of the armed services and encourage and empower those who have a desire to explore and engage in entrepreneurial-based livelihoods. They use a "mentoring" model to accomplish their work. What a great way for leaders to enjoin with and share their time and talent. In these situations, you often wonder who benefits more. This is the beauty of compassion and caring. It contributes to the lives of those involved—true fellowship results, and all are enriched.

Programs are available that focus on creation care, programs promoting justice and peace, character-building youth groups, animal protection, education, the arts, angel investment, microlending, and many more issues. They would welcome your interest and support.

"Do your giving while you're living so you're knowing where it's going."
—Edie Fraser and Robyn Spizman[17]

17 *Do Your Giving While You Are Living*--Morgan James Publishing, November 1, 2008. Where your sacrifices are given and your money is spent is the true barometer of your heart and generosity.

U

"U"

is for

"Us"

Us

"Who Is Better Than You?"—"Us!"

The answer "Us!" is, at its heart, an affirmation of effective leadership. It is evidence that there is a commitment to a common bond.

A leader must coalesce unique individuals into a body that becomes united in its purposes and endeavors as it works toward the goals and visions set forth before it. A leader must then remain in good conscience and be intentional to see that each individual is thriving and achieving, and that the group remains motivated and in a state of growth and creative endeavor.

A leader strives to gather, equip, and assign roles that best ensure that each individual thrives and achieves. Motivating, recognizing, and rewarding proficiency are all in the must-do purview of a leader.

Ultimately, a leader's success depends on his ability to unify and direct each member of a gathering to a sincere understanding and commitment that "us" is a much more rewarding and profitable state of being than "me."

V

"V"
is for
"Virtues and Values"

Virtues and Values

Consider the following definitions:

VIRTUE: behavior showing high moral standards

VALUE: a person's principles or standards of behavior; one's judgment of what is important in life.

Earnestly striving for, and incorporating, solid, morally based values and virtues into your life and entrepreneurial endeavors is your most essential task. From its platform spring your ideals, ideas, decisions, and actions. Through their employ, your resulting character, affect, and actions will influence every relationship you have and will speak volumes to those related parties and be a model worthy of being copied by others.

In my experience and research, I have focused on the work of those who ascribe to a science known as "Positive Psychology." Two of the most respected voices in this field are Christopher Peterson and Martin Siegelman. Together they developed the Values in Action Inventory of Strengths. Quoting Wikipedia:

The VIA Inventory of Strengths (VIA-IS), formally known as the "Values in Action" Inventory, is a proprietary psychological assessment measure designed to identify an individual's profile of character strengths. It was created in order to operationalize their Character Strengths and Virtues Handbook (CSV). The CSV is the positive psychology counterpart to the Diagnostic and Statistical Manual of Mental Disorders (DSM) used in traditional psychology. Unlike the DSM, which scientifically categorizes human deficits and disorders, the CSV classifies positive human strengths. This aligns with the overall goal of the positive psychology movement, which aims to make people's lives more fulfilling, rather than simply treating mental illness. Notably, the VIA-IS is the tool by which people can identify their own positive strengths and learn how to capitalize on them.

Classification of Strengths

1. Wisdom and Knowledge: creativity, curiosity, judgment, love of learning, perspective

2. Courage: bravery, perseverance, honesty, zest

3. Humanity: love, kindness, social intelligence

4. Justice: teamwork, fairness, leadership

5. Temperance: forgiveness, humility, prudence, self-regulated

6. Transcendence: appreciation of beauty and excellence[18]

For those who choose to answer the call to lead, it is paramount that the most significant life principle, character trait, and value they must embrace is honesty. Honesty is the value that as practiced provides the path of episodes and situations during which followers observe and come to trust in the leaders whom they see to be truthful. Demanding respect and the recognition of your authority is certainly an option, but trust that is earned is solid and unshakable.

The synonyms of "honest" provide an apt definition indeed— truthful, sincere, candid, frank, direct, open, forthright, and straight.

"Honesty is the best policy." In an era of spinning, fake news, social media, and rampant rationale this adage is still telling and wise. In the final assessment of matters, honesty is the most productive, kind, and efficient tact to take.

A leader must accept the responsibility that in word and deed he needs to seek, acknowledge, and speak the truth and be honest.

18 Wikipedia citation: https://en.wikipedia.org/wiki/Values_in_Action_Inventory_of_Strengths

His word must be his bond. Promised confidences, pledges honored, and debts paid are vows that a leader must embrace as his ethical mandate and platform.

These stresses are particularly poignant when the relationship is a close friend or family member. The tension between loving someone unconditionally versus sharing your thoughts candidly and being mindful that they may be offended or hurt by them is a dynamic I still need to resolve in my life.

Referring back to our discussion of the classification of strengths, be reminded that honesty is coupled along with bravery, perseverance, and zest—all traits under the inclusive word courage. The quest for and ability to be courageous is arduous. It demands great will and hard work. If it were not so, everybody would have it! A leader must push through the human condition of avoidance and combat the tug of yielding to cowardice and risk aversion.

In my own life, I struggle to be the forthright and honest person I aim to be. I am a first-born people pleaser! I want everyone to like me. I avoid negative-centric conversations and conflict. It stresses me to discipline or engage in constructive criticism.

I do not want to disappoint people or discourage them. I want to empower and encourage. I am gradually learning how to do both; they can be mutually inclusive.

When relationships must be dealt with honestly and openly, I take some time to reflect on the Golden Rule: "Treat others as you would want to be treated." This establishes for me a mindset of care and consideration for the parties involved and guides my thoughts and decisions, as well as colors the demeanor and character of the conversation. I often request of the party I am engaging with to permit the opportunity to introduce and expand on my thoughts for a period and, in so doing, have them understand that the topic is important to me and I have taken some time to be thoughtful and concerned. I assure them that my topic might be unsettling and unwelcome but that I share reflections grounded in care and have tried to "walk in their shoes" as I offer the content and the suggested resolve. I strive to be economical with my words but am certain to include justifications as appropriate, suggested solutions, and time frames going forward. My goal is to build on the trust I have with a person I am with and have them be confident in that I have their best interest at heart.

Witnessed honesty builds trust. A trusted leader is the core of a cohesive enterprise and the cornerstone of its success.

My earliest training as a leader occurred when I became patrol leader to seven boys in my group. As a scout, you pledge to be "trustworthy, loyal, helpful, friendly, courteous, kind, obedient, cheerful, thrifty, brave, clean, and reverent" as stated by the Boy Scouts Law.

Trustworthiness is the first law, for it is primal to all the others. Scouts learn that they are to tell the truth. They are to be honest and keep their promises. They are to do this because people depend on them. What a phenomenal litany for young leaders in training to recite, memorize, and put into practice in their lives.

W

"W"
is for
"Wellness"

Wellness and Well-being

Consider the following acrostic for the word well-being:

WALK three miles a day while meditating, praying, or reciting positive affirmations.

EAT three, modest proportioned meals prepared from fresh natural foods before 7:00pm.

LIQUIDATE! Water only; flavor with real fruit if desired.

LIVE each day with a plan and a balanced schedule. Include some times to breathe properly.

BED by a 10:00pm, with no devices!

ENJOY a glass of your favorite red wine daily.

INVESTIGATE or learn something new every day.

NOTHING really matters! Stay calm; be at peace.

GATHER together often with others for fun.

I highly recommend the website www.ontargetliving.com. This is the work of Chris Johnson. His programs are reasoned, rational, and extremely well thought out. I find his thinking to be very accommodating to time burdened leaders.

Imagine 250 years ago how Ben Franklin remarked on wellness and dieting when he suggested this: "To lengthen thy life, lessen thy meals!"

X

"X"
is for
"eXtra"

1 Percent Xtra

Read the poster on the following page thoughtfully. It is intriguing to ponder that an increase in just 1° of temperature (1/211th or .47%—less than half a percent) changes water from just very hot to steam. The use of steam and the power it generates has impacted, and continues to impact, our world and its progress in significant ways.

For me this poster speaks to the many traits entrepreneurs practice that illuminate their willingness to always employ extra effort—the "just one more time" that it takes to succeed. They will give whatever it takes.

There is no yield or limit in the mind of an entrepreneur.

In previous chapters we have spoken of persistence, drive, motivation, and hard work, etc. This poster sums it all up in one thought—just a little bit more can make all the difference.

> "Our greatest weakness lies in giving up. The most certain way to succeed is always to try just one more time."
> —Thomas Edison

> "It does not matter how slow you go as long as you do not stop."
> —Confucius

> "Be patient, even if every possibility seems closed."
> —Rumi

> "Leadership is encouraging average people to achieve above-average results with extra effort and energy."
> —General Colin Powell

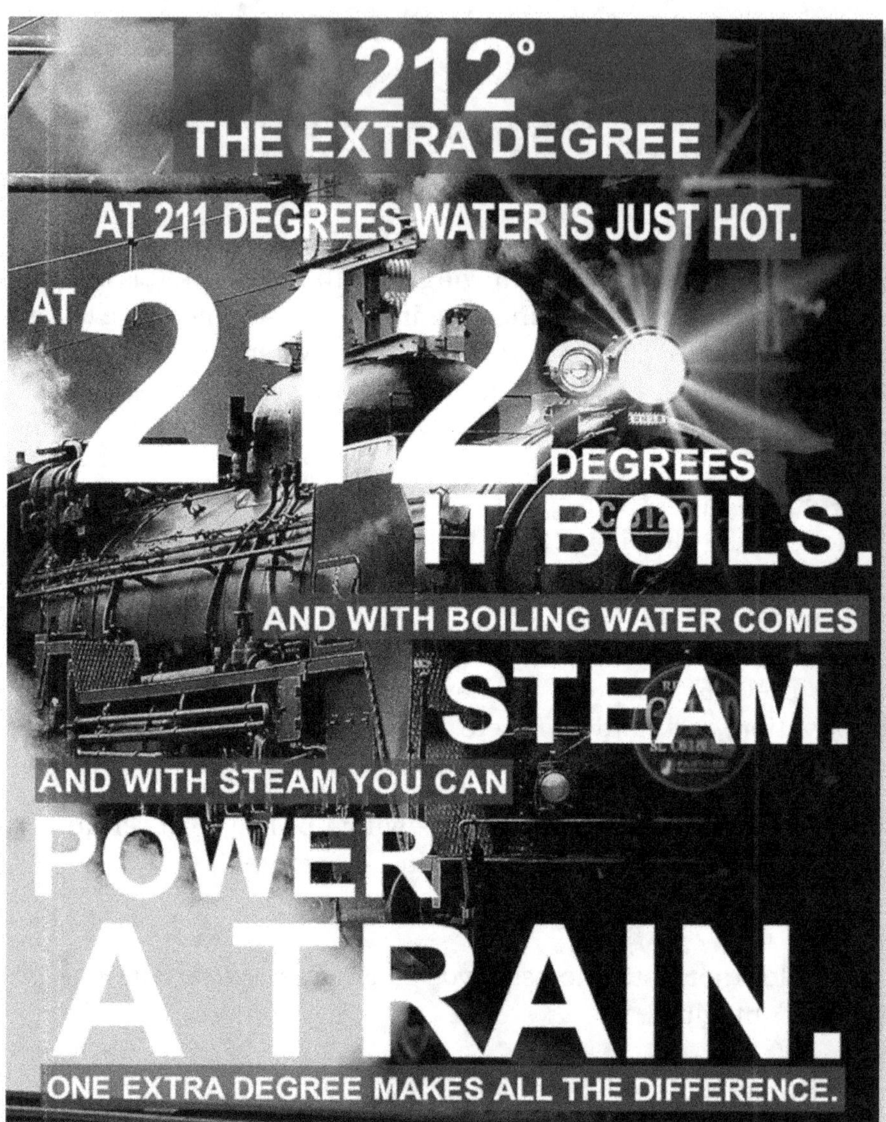
212°
THE EXTRA DEGREE
AT 211 DEGREES WATER IS JUST HOT.
AT 212° DEGREES
IT BOILS.
AND WITH BOILING WATER COMES
STEAM.
AND WITH STEAM YOU CAN
POWER A TRAIN.
ONE EXTRA DEGREE MAKES ALL THE DIFFERENCE.

Y

"Y"
is for
"YOLO"

YOLO

You Only Live Once

I urge you to live exuberantly, with excitement and energy. You only get one shot at this! I offer now a few quotations and writings of some very insightful people. Take special care to attend to the common threads of thought and insights. There is life wisdom in these words. Be encouraged. Be inspired.

"The two greatest days of your life are your birthday and the day you know why."
—Mark Twain

What I Know for Sure[19]

Everyone has the power for greatness—not for fame but greatness, because greatness is determined by service." Even before I first heard my all-time favorite quote from Dr. Martin Luther King, Jr., I knew in my heart that the message was true. As far back as I can recall, my prayer has been the same: "Use me, God. Show me how to take who I am, who I want to be, and what I can do, and use it for a purpose greater than myself."

All of us need a vision for our lives and even as we work to achieve the vision, we must surrender it to the power that is greater than we know. It's one of the defining principles of my life that I love to share: God can dream a bigger dream for you than you could ever dream for yourself. Before I understood that, I used to dream of having a salary to match my age—at 22, when I was earning $22,000 a year, I remember thinking that if I could just keep it up, I'd be making $40,000 by age 40. But the universe had a bigger dream for me, as it does for everyone reading these words. Success comes when you surrender to that dream—and let it lead you to the next best place.

What I know for sure is that if you want to have success, you can't make success your goal. As my friend Wintley Phipps, the gospel singer and minister, once told me, the key is not to worry about being successful but to instead work toward being significant—and the success will naturally flow. How can you serve your way to greatness? When you shift your focus from success to service, your work as a teacher, clerk, doctor, or dot-comer will instantly have more meaning.

We live in a world that confuses financial prosperity with success, dollars with the real deal of having a joy-filled life. By the late eighties I have achieved fame, notoriety, Emmys, money, houses with lots of things to put in them. I was prosperous, and yet a burning question nagged at me: What does all this mean? I've learned that possessions only have the meaning you give them. All my life, I'd been passing others big homes and yachts while wondering, What kind of person do you have to be to have all of that? Now I know that if you'll just be yourself and follow your calling, success will light itself before you in ways you never imagined. That doesn't mean we're all going to be yachting cross-country. Real success means creating a life of meaning through service that fulfills your reason for being here.

Starting today, you can decide to have a life of significance by how you give of yourself to others. In his book *The Soul's Code*, James Hillman says that the way to true success is to honor your calling. Have the courage to follow your passion—and if you don't know what it is, realize that one reason for your existence on earth is to find it. It won't come to you through some special announcement or through a burning bush. Your life's work is to find your life's work—and then to exercise the discipline, tenacity, and hard work it takes to pursue it.

How do you know whether you're on the right path, with the right person, or in the right job? The same way you know when you are not. You feel it. Each of us has a personal call to greatness—and because yours is as unique to you as your fingerprint, no one can tell you what it is.

Ignoring your passion is like dying a slow death. Your life is speaking to you every day, all the time—and your job is to listen up and find the clues. Passion whispers to you through your feelings, beckoning you toward your highest good. Pay attention to what makes you feel energized, connected, stimulated—what gives you your juice. Do what you love, give it back in the form of service, and you will do more than succeed. You will triumph.

Much can be gleaned from the commencement speech Steve Jobs gave on June 12, 2005. The following are a few quotes that speak of life and making decisions as to how to spend it.

When I was seventeen, I read a quote that went something like this: "If you live each day as if it was your last, someday you almost certainly will be right." It made an impression on me, and since then, for the past thirty-three years, I have looked in the mirror every morning and asked myself: "If today was the last day of my life, would I want to do what I'm doing today?" Remembering that I will be dead soon is the most important tool I've encountered to help me make the big choices in life. Because almost everything—all external expectations, all pride, all fear of embarrassment or failure—those things fall away in the face of death, leaving only what is truly important. Remembering that you are going to die is the best way I know to avoid the trap of thinking you have something to lose. You are already naked. . . . There's no reason not to follow your heart.

No one wants to die. Even people who want to go to

heaven don't want to die to get there. And yet death is the destination we all share. No one has ever escaped it. And that is as it should be, because death is very likely the single best invention in life. It is life's change agent.

Your time is limited, so don't waste it living someone else's life. Don't be trapped by dogma—which is living with the results of other people's thinking. Don't let the noise of others' opinions drown out your own inner voice. And most important, have the courage to follow your heart and intuition. They somehow already know what you truly want to become, everything else is secondary.

"The purpose of life is to engage in disciplined action for the sole intent of doing good."
—Jay Belding

"The *gift* of life is experienced by staying in the *present*!"
— Jay Belding

"Most people are as happy as they make up their minds to be."
—Abraham Lincoln

"Happiness lies in the joy of achievements and the thrill of creative effort."
—Franklin D. Roosevelt

"Stay Happy—Stay Foolish."
—Last words of the last issue of the Whole Earth Catalog

"We make a living by what we get, but we make in life by what we give."
—Winston Churchill

Dr. Jordan B. Peterson, a professor at Harvard and the University of Toronto, has recently written a compelling book entitled *12 Rules for Life: An Antidote to Chaos*. It is equal parts philosophy, psychology, and self-help book. It covers a broad range of topics drawling from life experiences, religion, and history. It offers great advice. "Order is truth," Dr. Peterson declares.

The Table of Contents of *12 Rules for Life*

- RULE 1 Stand up straight with your shoulders back
- RULE 2 Treat yourself like someone you are responsible for helping
- RULE 3 Make friends with people who want the best for you
- RULE 4 Compare yourself to who you were yesterday, not to who someone else is today
- RULE 5 Do not let your children do anything that makes you dislike them
- RULE 6 Set your house in perfect order before you criticize the world
- RULE 7 Pursue what is meaningful (not what is expedient)
- RULE 8 Tell the truth—or, at least, don't lie
- RULE 9 Assume that the person you are listening to might know something you don't
- RULE 10 Be precise in your speech
- RULE 11 Do not bother children when they are skateboarding
- RULE 12 Pet a cat when you encounter one on the street

"Recent research in social psychology has shown that happy people are not people who have more; rather, they are people who are happy with what they already have. Happy people engage in 'satisficing' (definition—to accept an available option as satisfactory) all of the time, even if they don't know it."
—Daniel Leviton

How to Be Happy

Robert Louis Stevenson (1850-1894)

1. Make up your mind to be happy. Learn to find pleasure in simple things.

2. Make the best of your circumstances. No one has everything, and everyone has something of sorrow intermingled with gladness in life. The trick is to make the laughter outweigh the tears.

3. Don't take yourself too seriously. Don't think that somehow you should be protected from misfortune that befalls other people.

4. You can't please everybody. Don't let criticism worry you.

5. Don't let your neighbor set your standards. Be yourself.

6. Do the things you enjoy doing but stay out of debt.

7. Never borrow trouble. Imaginary things are harder to bear then real ones.

8. Since hate poisons the soul, do not cherish jealousy, enmity, grudges. Avoid people who make you unhappy.

9. Have many interests. If you can't travel, read about new places.

10. Don't hold post-mortems. Don't spend your time brooding over sorrows or mistakes. Don't be one who never gets over things.

11. Do what you can for those less fortunate than yourself.

12. Keep busy at something. A busy person never has time to be unhappy.

"Finish each day and be done with it. You have done what you could, some blunders and absurdities have crept in; forget them as soon as you can. Tomorrow is a new day. You shall begin it serenely and with too high a spirit to be encumbered with your old nonsense,"
—Ralph Waldo Emerson

The Serenity Prayer

"God grant me the serenity to accept the things I cannot change, courage to change the things I can, and the wisdom to know the difference."
—Reinhold Niebuhr, written in 1932

What Will Matter

A Poem by Michael Josephson

Ready or not, someday it will all come to an end.

All the things you collected whether treasure or baubles will pass to someone else.

There will be no more surprises, no minutes, hours, or days.

Your wealth, fame, and temporal power will shrivel to irrelevance. It will not matter what you own or what you were owed.

Your grudges, resentments, frustrations, and jealousies will finally disappear. So, too, your hopes, ambitions, plans, and to do lists will expire.

The wins and losses that once seemed important will fade away. It won't matter where you came from or what side of the tracks you lived, at the end.

It won't matter whether you were beautiful or brilliant. Even your gender and skin color will be irrelevant.

So what will matter? How will the value of your days be measured?

What will matter is not what you bought, but what you built; not what you got, but what you gave.

What will matter is not your success, but your significance. What will matter is not what you learned, but what you taught.

What will matter is every act of integrity, compassion, or sacrifice that enriched, empowered or encouraged others to emulate your example.

What will matter is not your competence, but your character.

What will matter is not how many people you knew, but how many people will feel a lasting loss, when you're gone.

What will matter is the clarity and care at which you have loved others, and have been a positive influence in their lives.

What will matter is not your memories, but the memories that live in those who love you.

What will matter is how long you will be remembered by whom and for what.

Living a life that matters doesn't happen by accident. It's not a matter of circumstances but of choice.

When you receive something so beautiful as this, you must not hesitate to share it with your friends.
God, I want to take a minute, not to ask for anything from You but simply say thank you for all I have.

Mother Teresa's Business Card

No one returned emptyhanded from Mother Teresa. She would press a metal of the Virgin Mary into the palm of the person's hands, or a piece of paper with a prayer which she said, or a quotation from the Holy Bible. These she would autograph if asked to do so, no matter how pressed she was for time.

The pile of business cards handed to Mother Teresa in return, if placed one on top of the other, would have reached heaven! But Mother herself had no "business" card and it did not cross her mind until one day, a businessman who met her briefly and wanted to contact her again, asked, "Mother, may I have your business card?" Mother delved into the cloth bag with wooden handles that she carried when traveling and handed him a prayer card. He looked at it and asked again, "Mother, don't you have a business card?"

Mother thought about the gentleman's question and late one night, she wrote out her own "business" in five lines:

The fruit of SILENCE is Prayer
The fruit of PRAYER is Faith
The fruit of FAITH is Love
The fruit of LOVE is Service
The fruit of SERVICE is Peace
Mother Teresa

Desiderata

GO PLACIDLY amid the noise and the haste, and remember what peace there may be in silence. As far as possible, without surrender, be on good terms with all persons.
Speak your truth quietly and clearly; and listen to others, even to the dull and the ignorant; they too have their story. Avoid loud and aggressive persons; they are vexatious to the spirit. If you compare yourself with others, you may become vain or bitter, for always there will be greater and lesser persons than yourself.
Enjoy your achievements as well as your plans. Keep interested in your own career, however humble; it is a real possession in the changing fortunes of time.
Exercise caution in your business affairs, for the world is full of trickery. But let this not blind you to what virtue there is; many persons strive for high ideals, and everywhere life is full of heroism.
Be yourself. Especially do not feign affection. Neither be cynical about love; for in the face of all aridity and disenchantment, it is as perennial as the grass.

Take kindly the counsel of the years, gracefully surrendering the things of youth.

Nurture strength of spirit to shield you in sudden misfortune. But do not distress yourself with dark imaginings. Many fears are born of fatigue and loneliness.

Beyond a wholesome discipline, be gentle with yourself. You are a child of the universe no less than the trees and the stars; you have a right to be here.

And whether or not it is clear to you, no doubt the universe is unfolding as it should. Therefore be at peace with God, whatever you conceive Him to be. And whatever your labors and aspirations, in the noisy confusion of life, keep peace in your soul. With all its sham, drudgery and broken dreams, it is still a beautiful world. Be cheerful. Strive to be happy.[20]

Philippians 4:10-13

Christian psychiatrists Frank Minirth and Paul Meier have some suggestions for practicing contentment:

- JUST FOR TODAY I will try to live through this day only, not tackling my whole life problem at once.

- JUST FOR TODAY I will try to be happy, realizing my happiness does not depend on what others do or say, or what happens around me. Happiness is a result of being at peace with myself.

- JUST FOR TODAY I will try to adjust myself to what is and not force everything to adjust to my own desires. I will accept my family, my friends, my business, my circumstances as they come.

- JUST FOR TODAY I will do at least one thing I don't want to do, and I will perform some small act of love for my neighbor.

- JUST FOR TODAY I will have a quiet time of meditation wherein I shall think of God, myself, and my neighbor. I shall

---

20 By Max Ehrmann © 1927; Original text

relax and seek truth. JUST FOR TODAY I shall be unafraid to be happy, enjoy what is good, what is beautiful, and what is lovely in life.

- JUST FOR TODAY I will accept myself and live to the best of my ability. JUST FOR TODAY I choose to believe that I can live this one day.[21]

The Prayer of St. Francis

St. Francis of Assisi (1182-1226)

Lord, make me an instrument of your peace
Where there is hatred, let me sow love
Where there is injury, pardon
Where there is doubt, faith
Where there is despair, hope
Where there is darkness, light
And where there is sadness, joy

Oh Divine Master, grant that I may
Not so much seek to be consoled as to console
To be understood, as to understand
To be loved, as to love
For it is in giving that we receive
And it's in pardoning that we are pardoned
And it's in dying that we are born to Eternal Life

21 Program: The Secret of Contentment Tape TH232

The Paradoxical Commandments

by Dr. Kent M. Keith

People are illogical, unreasonable, and self-centered.
Love them anyway.

If you do good, people will accuse you of selfish ulterior motives.
Do good anyway.

If you are successful, you will win false friends and true enemies.
Succeed anyway.

The good you do today will be forgotten tomorrow.
Do good anyway.

Honesty and frankness make you vulnerable.
Be honest and frank anyway.

The biggest men and women with the biggest ideas can be shot
down by the smallest men and women with the smallest minds.
Think big anyway.

People favor underdogs but follow only top dogs.
Fight for a few underdogs anyway.

What you spend years building may be destroyed overnight.
Build anyway.

People really need help but may attack you if you do help them.
Help people anyway.

Give the world the best you have and you'll get kicked in the teeth.
Give the world the best you have anyway.

The Secret to Happiness

The secret to happiness and well-being is no mystery. All it takes is the ability to do the following:

- Forget.
- Apologize.
- Admit errors.
- Avoid mistakes.
- Listen to advice.
- Keep your temper.
- Shoulder the blame.
- Make the best of things.
- Maintain high standards.
- Think first and act accordingly.
- Put the needs of others before your own.
- Forgive.

Seem like a tall order? Then try slipping as many of these "secrets to happiness" into your day as possible. You'll soon be rewarded with a more positive outlook on life.

Words of Lasting Value to Any Manager

By: Bill Marriot Sr./Founder Marriot Hotels
. . . to his son who replaced him as CEO[22]

1. Keep physically, mentally and spiritually strong.

2. Guard your habits—bad ones will destroy you.

3. Pray about every difficult problem.

4. Study and follow professional management principles.

5. People are No. 1—their development, loyalty, interest, team spirit. Develop managers and every area.

6. Decisions: people grow making decisions and assuming responsibility for them.

- Make crystal clear what decision each manager is responsible for and what decisions you reserved for yourself.

- Have all the facts and counsel necessary—then decide and stick to it.

7. Criticism: Don't criticize people but make a fair appraisal of their qualifications with their supervisor only (or someone assigned to do this).

8. Remember, anything you say about someone may (and usually does) get back to them. There are few secrets.

9. See the good in people and try to develop these qualities.

10. Inefficiency: If it cannot be overcome and an employee is obviously incapable of the job, find a job he can do or terminate *now*. Don't wait.

11. Manage your time.

- Short conversations—to the point.

- Make every minute on the job count.

- Work fewer hours—some of us waste half our time.

---

22 Marriott's Portfolio: Fall 1986, 56.

12. Delegate and hold accountable for results.

13. Details:

- Let your staff take care of them.

- Save your energy for planning, thinking, working with department heads, promoting new ideas.

- Don't do anything someone else can do for you.

14. Ideas in competition:

- Ideas keep the business alive.

- Know what your competitors are doing and planning.

- Encourage all management to think about better ways and give suggestions on anything that will improve business.

- Spend time and money on research and development.

15. Don't try to do an employee's job for him—counsel and suggest.

16. Think objectively and keep a sense of humor. Make the business fun for you and others.

What I Know for Sure

By Jay Belding

- Strive to live your life each moment as if you want someone to share it at your funeral.

- The joy of living a life with an entrepreneurial mind and spirit is that you are conscious of the greatest paradox of life—it is better to give than to receive.

- The key to life is contentment. Having a giving spirit yields contentment, the key to it is to realize that our sole (soul) purpose is to nurture and protect all of those we are in a relationship with, especially all those we have not met yet.

- People are our passion. We live focused on our mission to warm our heart by warming the hearts of others; by serving and giving them opportunity, substance, employ, power, and a sense of worthiness; in a word; dignity.

- Do good; and you will do well.

- Strive to be generous, never thinking about the "cost" or getting paid back.

- The Beatles, "And in the end, the love you take is equal to the love you make." Amen

Now you write,
What I know for sure by:

____

Your Name

Z

"Z"
is for
"Zest"

Zest

Zest is regarded as a component of the virtue of courage. Zest is defined as living life with a sense of excitement, anticipation, and energy. Zest is approaching life as an adventure—in such a way that one is motivated by challenging situations and tasks. One makes lemonade from the lemons!

My closing sentiment is that I encourage you to embark on a quest to be passionate in all of your endeavors and with the people in your life. With love, lead all those you are connected to so that they feel dignified and have a reason to be grateful that you touched their lives. May your mantra be "Who is better than you? Us!"

Go forth courageously, with zest, my friend! Amen

About the Author

Jay Belding grew up with five siblings in Northern New Jersey in a bedroom community of New York City.

He received a Bachelor of Science Degree in Industrial Arts and Technology in 1972, and a Master's in Special Education in 1973—both from Trenton State College; now the College of New Jersey.

Jay was a special education teacher focusing on vocational training with the Bucks County Public Schools in Pennsylvania from 1973 to 1977. During his tenure he was a classroom teacher; a supervisor for eight classrooms; directed a job placement program; and he wrote, developed, and implemented an innovative vocation education curriculum for special education students.

He cofounded Jon-Jay builders in 1979, a residential construction company. After five projects he sold his interest to his partner in 1979.

In 1977, along with his wife, he founded, and to this day is the Executive Director of Associated Production Services Incorporated (www.apspackage.com), a 501 C-3, not for profit, state of Pennsylvania certified vocational training facility. APS operates six workshop centers serving 500 developmentally disabled adults with a staff of 105. The training and work engaged in is via packaging contracts awarded by companies primarily in the confectionary and food business. Some assembly and packaging of consumer goods is also performed. APS is registered with the FDA and SQF regulatory bodies.

He co-founded, and was a partner, in Magna–Board, Inc. This company manufactured and purveyed magnetic, decorative framed boards to the gift and stationary trade. He sold interest to his partner in 1983.

Jay founded and owned Regency Candle Company in 1980, which produced and sold a complete line of gift store quality candles through a national team of manufacturers' representatives. There was also a container-filling division and wholesale division in the company. The product line expanded to include decorative iron accessories as well as silk and plastic rings and wreaths. Regency was sold in 1986.

Country Kitchen Cookies Inc. was acquired in 1981 through a barter-based marketing agreement with the owner. The company was sold in 1985.

Jay became a partner and Director of Operations of the New York Style Bagel Chip Company Inc., in 1984. The Business was sold to Nabisco in 1992.

He founded and owned Premium Pet Company Inc., in 1982, which trademarked and manufactured two primary items—Disposa Scoop and Disposa Tray for cat litter removal. This business was acquired in 1990.

In 2010, Jay designed and trademarked Ergo Bagstand®, a user-friendly large trash bag holder for commercial/industrial applications. This business is a going concern to this day.

In 2013, he founded a product line of bag sealing devices. Under the names Bag Tie® and Bag Tite® these durable, reusable bag closures keep food fresh. The concept is that of a "tin tie," such as the closure on a bag of Starbucks coffee. It is sold primarily through private label programs in large grocery chains.

Civic Activities

- Ruling Elder at Doylestown Presbyterian Church, Doylestown Pennsylvania.

- Served on the Board of Directors of Riverside Symphonia, Life Abundant Ministries, and Heritage Land Conservancy—all in Bucks County, Pennsylvania.

- Coached boys and girls travel soccer teams.

- Scoutmaster Troop 12 in Trenton, New Jersey, in 1972, and Troop 29 in Buckingham, Pennsylvania from 1993-1998.

Jay currently resides in Pennsylvania with his wife, Barbara. They enjoy their time spent with their two children and their families—especially their three delightful grandchildren.